The Sacred Prostitute

Marie-Louise von Franz, Honorary Patron

**Studies in Jungian Psychology
by Jungian Analysts**

Daryl Sharp, General Editor

The Sacred Prostitute

Eternal Aspect of the Feminine

NANCY QUALLS-CORBETT

With a Foreword by
MARION WOODMAN

Many people have encouraged my research for this work. Among them are Suzanne, Peter, Martha, Virginia, Harold, Eleanor, Sherry, Eugene, Stefanie, Valerie, Larry, my analysands and particularly my husband Gene. I thank them all and especially Maurice.

Canadian Cataloguing in Publication Data

Qualls-Corbett, Nancy
   The sacred prostitute

(Studies in Jungian psychology by Jungian analysts; 32)

Bibliography: p.
Includes index.

ISBN 0-919123-31-7

1. Prostitution—Religious aspects.   2. Femininity (Psychology).
3. Sex—Religious aspects.   4. Jung, C.G. (Carl Gustav), 1875-1961.
I. Title. II. Series.

HQ61.Q35 1988   155.3   C87-095225-0

INNER CITY BOOKS
Box 1271, Station Q, Toronto, Canada M4T 2P4
Telephone (416) 927-0355

Honorary Patron: Marie-Louise von Franz.
Publisher and General Editor: Daryl Sharp.
Business Development: Vicki Cowan.
Editorial Board: Fraser Boa, Daryl Sharp, Marion Woodman.
Production Assistants: Ben Sharp, David Sharp.

INNER CITY BOOKS was founded in 1980 to promote the understanding and practical application of the work of C.G. Jung.

Cover: Seated Nude, 1884, oil painting by A. W. Bouguereau (1825-1905).
© 1982 Sterling and Francine Clark Art Institute, Williamstown, Mass.

Index by Daryl Sharp.

Printed and bound in Canada by Webcom Limited

Contents

See final pages for descriptions of other Inner City Books

Acknowledgments

The Black Madonna, unpublished manuscript by Giles Quispel. All rights reserved.

"Suzanne" by Leonard Cohen, © copyright 1966, Project Seven Music, div. CTMP Inc., 120 Charles St., New York, NY 10014. All rights reserved.

"I Don't Know How to Love Him," and "Everything's Alright," lyrics by Tim Rice, music by Andrew Lloyd Webber, © copyright 1969 by Leeds Music Corporation, New York, NY 10019. All rights reserved.

Foreword

Marion Woodman

Nancy Qualls-Corbett asked herself the very question that many of us must be asking when we pick up this book: "What is it in me that is drawn to the sacred prostitute?"

To our modern minds, the words themselves seem contradictory. "Sacred" suggests dedication to a divine spirit; "prostitute" suggests defilement of the human body. How can the two words be related when mind is separated from matter, spirituality from sexuality? The mystery of this paradox is the subject of this book. Its potential for healing is crucial to many floundering relationships.

Today, when a man falls in love with his perfect woman, he projects onto her attributes of the divine mother: beauty, goodness, chastity, life-giving love. She in turn projects onto him attributes of the divine father: loyalty, power, virility, the Rock of Gibraltar at the center of her life. In the beginning, love and lust are one in their unconscious Garden of Paradise.

When reality creeps into that Garden—often after the marriage ceremony—the projections begin to shatter. The man may feel himself strangling in the noose of his partner's expectations; her very goodness then evokes his guilt as he fantasizes freedom with a "real woman" who can receive him as a "real man." While he loves his "perfect" mother, at the same time he seeks to escape her dark side, the devouring witch to whom he can never give enough. She, insecure in her own womanhood and sensing his withdrawal, finds herself clinging like a rejected child to a father who is pulling away.

Trapped in their love (or neurotic dependence), one or both may find another, less perfect, partner with whom to have a relationship that is more human, more lusty, with fewer strings attached. This split may hold for a long time. Within the split, however, lie rage, expressed or repressed, and a profound yearning for total union.

If consciousness is introduced into the situation, the cause of the disturbance may become clear. In dreams, for example, the woman may suddenly become mother in the marriage bed, the man become father. In bringing their bodies to conscious awareness, women often discover they cannot surrender to sexual penetration. They realize they are either mother to their husband-son, or daughter to their husband-father. In both situations, their body says no to incest. However dearly they may love their husband in spirit, their matter rejects the unconscious relationship. Then a period of celibacy can lead to sexual and spiritual integration.

Now, as men are becoming more conscious, their matter is likewise rejecting incest with mother or daughter, and their impotence is propelling them to a new level of relationship in which mature man unites with mature woman. It is a time of intense anguish for both men and women, a time that demands patience, courage and fearsome honesty.

In my analytic practice, I am constantly faced with dream images that each sex is unconsciously projecting onto the other. Centuries of repressed rage manifest in dreams of cutting off dictators' heads, arms, genitalia. Centuries of grief appear in images of feminine sacrifice on monolithic rocks or dining room tables. The unconscious battle of the sexes is one thing; the conscious battle is far more painful, far more bitter. The rage and grief are in the dreams of both men and women who are becoming conscious of their ravaged femininity.

In addition, sensitive men are facing their personal grief for the patriarchy's betrayal of the feminine. Sensitive women are facing the wall lodged in their own bodies—a wall that stands adamant against penetration and spiritual surrender. The fear of being penetrated, in both sexes, is no less than the fear of penetrating.

Many physical illnesses erupt when this fear becomes conscious and cannot be overcome in the life situation. Dream images of creatures that are part human, part animal—terrified creatures that scuttle about the bedroom—leave the dreamer deeply disturbed. The possibility of masculine and feminine uniting in harmony seems to fade into darkness.

The light of the sacred prostitute penetrates to the heart of this darkness. As so vividly described by Nancy Qualls-Corbett, she is the consecrated priestess in the temple, spiritually receptive to the feminine power flowing through her from the Goddess, and at the same time joyously aware of the beauty and passion in her human body. Surrendered to the cosmic energies of love, she magnifies the Goddess in physical delight and spiritual ecstasy. She opens the masculine to the potency of penetrating to the divine, and the feminine to the rapture of surrender to it. The mystery of that union dwells beyond the finite bonds of personal love.

While contemplating the possibility of healing the split between sexuality and spirituality through connection with the sacred prostitute, modern men and women need also to contemplate the dangers. We are not at the same place in the evolution of human consciousness as were the ancient sacred prostitutes. Centuries of splitting spirit from matter have left us far from either the understanding or the experience of matter as sacred. Daily the earth is raped. Daily the wisdom of the human body is ravaged by the mind.

So long as we are unconscious of the divinity inherent in matter, sexuality can be manipulated to fulfill ego desire; the sacred prostitute is not present, nor is the Goddess being invoked. Instead of manifesting as a transformative power that can mediate between wounded instinct and the radiance of the divine, the Goddess is called upon to justify lust and sexual license.

Light does not come through incessant wallowing in the dark. All our rage, all our bitterness, all our fears, are stepping stones that lead through darkness into light. But they are merely stepping stones. Only from a clear vision of oneness, an experience of genuine love, can we live our own truth. Whether this experience is given through another human being or through a solitary connection with the divine, this is the experience that illumines our lives.

Astarte, Goddess of Love.
(Terracotta, Sumerian period; Louvre)

Introduction

For I am the first and the last.
I am the honored one and the scorned one.
I am the whore and the holy one.
I am the wife and the virgin.
I am (the mother) and the daughter.
I am the members of my mother. . . .
I am the silence that is incomprehensible
  and the idea whose remembrance is frequent.
I am the voice whose sound is manifold
  and the word whose appearance is multiple.
I am the utterance of my name.
—"The Thunder, Perfect Mind," *Nag Hammadi Library.*

On my first excursion to Israel several years ago, I noticed numerous little clay statues in the small gift shops of the kibbutzim and in the larger antique stores. I was attracted to these figures almost magnetically. Each had the form of a woman. Some were delicately molded while others were crudely formed; some depicted the entire body with intricate designs on the gown or headdress, others were simply fragments of a small head with only a suggestion of facial expression. They were not reproductions, they were originals dating back to long before the Common Era (B.C.E.).

Excavated from the ruins of many towns and villages of this ancient land, they were images of ancient goddesses. Because they were found in such great numbers, the Israeli government allowed those of less than museum quality to be sold and taken out of the country. They reminded me of James Michener's novel, *The Source,* which describes the excavation of the imaginary tell of Makor in eastern Galilee, a site reminiscent of the actual tell of Megiddo in north-central Israel, whose first city dates back to 3,500 B.C.E.

As the novel's archaeologists unearth artifacts which disclose practices of community life in the unrecorded civilizations piled high on the rubble of earlier societies, the author spins a story of the people and customs of the age in question. The small clay statues brought to mind a chapter in the book telling of the goddess Astarte.

In Makor, in 2202 B.C.E., a husky farmer, Urbaal, purchased this special statue of Astarte at great expense, although he already owned

11

three others. "She was six inches high," writes Michener, "nude, very feminine, with wide hips and hands cupped below circular breasts. She was erotic and plump, delightful to study and reassuring to have in one's presence."[1]

Urbaal worshiped Astarte, for it was she who could assure the fecundity of his land and his wives. It was through her powers that he might become the man chosen to lie with the beautiful ritual priestess in the temple of Astarte for seven days and nights, as was the custom during the religious feasts of thanksgiving. The priestess, a sacred prostitute, was tall and exquisitely beautiful,

> a perfection of the goddess Astarte, for no man could look at her provocative form without seeing in her the sublime representation of fertility. She was a girl whose purpose was to be loved, to be taken away and made fertile so that she could reproduce her grandeur and bless the earth.[2]

Holding the little goddess tenderly in his hands, Urbaal prayed for her intercession. "Help me, Astarte. Let it be me."

As ancient civilizations such as Urbaal's were destroyed, their clay images buried under ruins for eons, so were the gods and goddesses who protected and insured their growth. No longer did the sacred prostitute, the human woman who embodied the goddess, dance in the temple to excite the communication of body and soul. The temple of the goddess of love, no longer vital, went underground.

Who was "the sacred prostitute"? And what happened to the developing consciousness of humankind when people no longer venerated the goddess of love, passion and sex?

These questions bothered me. Much as I wanted to put them out of my head, they continued to jostle and nag me as if, almost autonomously, the sacred prostitute and her goddess wanted to be known. I felt compelled to investigate historical accounts of sacred prostitution, tthe goddess' role in the lives of ordinary people in ancient civilizations, and the sacred sexual ceremonies enacted in the temple of love. But most of all, I wanted to know what relevance these ancient rituals might have for men and women today.

In the course of my investigation, other questions emerged. What has happened to our understanding of the goddess, the divine femi-

---

[1] James A. Michener, *The Source,* p. 104.
[2] Ibid., p. 115.

nine, in contemporary times? Why is woman's sexuality so exploited, so debased, when once it was revered? How can men come to know and to value the deeper meaning of femininity? And why is sexuality cut off from spirituality, as if they were opposites?

This last question, in particular, claimed my attention. Listening to the stories men and women told me, I became increasingly aware that in their lives sexuality and spirituality were often in conflict, and sometimes both were absent.

As an analyst I saw many people who felt they were unloved, or even unworthy of being loved, and many who had altogether lost the capacity to love. I saw that the acquisition of material gains or power offered only false hopes of personal fulfillment. I observed that a person's spiritual search through the avenues of organized religion at times resulted in confusion, additional conflict, guilt and despair. This dis-ease was expressed in different ways: "I feel empty inside," someone would say; or, "My life has no meaning, I'm simply existing"; or, "My body is dead"; or even, "My soul is dead."

Inevitably, I related these statements to my research, to the questions that nagged at me. I began to see that the pervasive emptiness people complained of could be explained in terms of the loss of the goddess—the one who renews life, brings love, passion, fertility—and the sensuous priestess—the human woman who brought the attributes of the goddess into the lives of human beings. The connection to an important layer of instinctual life—joy, beauty, a creative energy that unites sexuality and spirituality—had been lost.

My observations were not restricted to the consulting room. The proliferation of substance dependency, physical abuse, sexual promiscuity, and living on the fast track in order not to feel the emptiness of one's life—all point to the loss of a vital element in life. Without superficial props, a certain dullness creeps in and we are confronted with the lack of personal resources which could engender a new sense of vitality.

Contemporary men and women, unlike Urbaal of ancient times, no longer have the opportunity to hold tenderly the little image of the goddess or become awe-inspired while viewing the sacred prostitute dancing in the temple, her beautiful body the representation of joy and passion. Without benefit of direct experience, we can know of the sacred prostitute only through reading deciphered cuneiform tablets or ancient manuscripts describing her rituals. The rational mind has simply relegated her to the category of "archaic pagan practices."

Indeed, the term "sacred prostitute" presents a paradox to our logical minds, for, as I have indicated, we are disinclined to associate that which is sexual with that which is consecrated to the gods. Thus the significance of this temple priestess escapes us, and we remain disconnected from an image that represents the vital, full-bodied nature of the feminine. Without this image, modern men and women continue to live out contemporary persona roles, never fully realizing the depth of emotion and fullness of life inherent in the feeling tone which surrounds the image of the sacred prostitute.

Much as the archaeological artifacts described by Michener revealed values of ancient civilizations, images from the deep recesses of our unconscious can enlighten us by disclosing aspects of ourselves which have been repressed or ignored. We bury these images when they create conflict with some conscious value or attitude; consequently we lose the meaning symbolized by them. New models or images take their place. As older images, such as the little clay statue symbolizing the communion of sexuality and spirituality, become inaccessible to our conscious understanding, so a source of vital energy escapes us.

In the body of psychological thought developed by C. G. Jung, such images are considered "archetypal." An archetype is a pre-existent form that is part of the inherited structure of the psyche common to all people.[3] These psychic structures are endowed with strong feeling tones. The archetype, as a psychic entity, is surrounded by energy which has the ability to activate and transform conscious contents. When the archetype is constellated, that is, activated, the release of that specific energy is recognized by consciousness and felt in the body through the emotions. Thus, for example, when the archetype of the goddess of love is constellated, we are imbued with the vitality of love, beauty, sexual passion and spiritual renewal.

Jung writes that the loss of an archetype "gives rise to that frightful 'discontent in our culture.'"[4] Without the vital feminine to balance

---

[3] "A Psychological View of Conscience," *Civilization in Transition*, CW 10, par. 847. [CW refers throughout to *The Collected Works of C.G. Jung*.] A more extensive discussion of archetypes appears below in chapter 2.

[4] "Concerning the Archetypes and the Anima Concept," *The Archetypes and the Collective Unconscious*, CW 9i, par. 141.

Clay goddesses.
(Cyprus, ca. 2500 B.C.; British Museum)

the collective patriarchal principle, there is a certain barrenness to life. Creativity and personal development are stifled.

When the divine feminine, the goddess, is no longer revered, social and psychic structures become overmechanized, overpoliticized, overmilitarized. Thinking, judgment and rationality become the ruling factors. The needs for relatedness, feeling, caring or attending to nature go unheeded. There is no balance, no harmony, neither within oneself nor in the external world. With the disregard of the archetypal image so related to passionate love, a splitting off of values, a one-sidedness, occurs in the psyche. As a result, we are sadly crippled in our search for wholeness and health.

As I began to appreciate these implications, not only for the individual but for society as a whole, another difficulty took shape. If the problem was the loss of certain aspects of the feminine archetype, then it was important to regain them. But how? Archaeological digs offered a wonderful model. Instead of digging deep in the earth to recover hidden treasures, I would "dig" in the dark, mysterious spaces of the unconscious to bring those dormant images to the light of consciousness.

The historical accounts I had read, and recorded laws dating from time immemorial, provided a framework, the basic data about the image for which I was searching. Information from universal literature, such as myths, fairy tales and religious documents, so rich in archetypal images and motifs, filled out the profile. As these stories told of characteristic traits and activities of the goddess, the image of the sacred prostitute took on more substance and a distinct personality. These sources gave me an understanding of the attributes of the goddess and her votary; I could then translate them, as it were, into psychological dynamics.

Most important in finding the relevance of the sacred prostitute to contemporary life were the symbolic images stemming from dreams, visions and fantasies, and from common life experiences, of modern men and women. The image of the sacred prostitute, which connects the essences of sexuality and spirituality, could be discerned in various ways as she appeared in each individual's unconscious material. It was interesting to see that once the image was made conscious, there was a noticeable change in the person's attitudes.

These separate steps of my investigation lent themselves to the format of this book. The historical accounts of the sacred prostitute are elaborated in the opening chapter, which then looks into the demise of sacred prostitution and the cultural and psychological changes which resulted. The second chapter discusses the general psychological significance of sacred prostitution. The third and fourth chapters describe the image of the sacred prostitute as it appears in dreams of men and women, respectively, and its meaning in terms of masculine and feminine psychology. The final chapter takes the image forward, as it were, exploring ways in which the vital powers of the goddess of love and the sacred prostitute might be reactivated in the lives of modern men and women.

The psychological orientation of this work is that of the Jungian school of thought, analytical psychology. Dream interpretation is based on the synthetic or constructive approach, in which symbolic expressions of the unconscious are amplified through archetypal images or motifs.

I do take exception with some of the teachings of Jung and his early male followers on the question of feminine nature. Their contributions deserve recognition, for they went against current beliefs in emphasizing the importance of the feminine to the health of the psyche; however, their point of view was essentially patriarchal. Certainly, at that time this point of view had not been widely contested, and it is understandable that Jung and other men viewed the feminine psyche according to their experience of what Jung called the anima, a man's inner image of woman.[5]

Writers like M. Esther Harding, an early advocate of Jungian thought, view the essence of feminine psychology in sharp contrast to masculine psychology. It is from the works of Harding and other women authors, mediated by my own experience, that I have distilled my image of the essential elements of the feminine nature.

Certain terms in this book, such as anima and animus, are more or less unique to Jung's psychology. These are defined as they appear. Where Jung refers to the feminine principle, I have chosen instead to speak of feminine nature—from Latin *natura,* meaning birth or the universe. "Nature" implies that which is inborn, real, not artificial; that is the meaning I wish to impart when speaking of the psychic nature of the feminine.

Where I refer to Eros, it is in the sense originally elaborated by Jung, describing the inner law of psychic energy which pertains to

---

[5] To his credit, Jung at least realized the propensity of men to project their anima onto women and wrote about the attendant consequences. See below, chapter 3.

relatedness, to joining, to mediating. My references to modern religious thought are concentrated on Western Christian tradition. Oriental and Near Eastern religious practices, although rich in symbolism relating to the sacred prostitute and the divine feminine, will not be discussed here (except for amplification in a few instances). By the same token there are many parallels in Oriental mythology, but my investigations have been limited to Western cultural mythology and early Middle Eastern mythology.

Included here are some case studies in which the image of the sacred prostitute was relevant. I realize that it is not pertinent in all cases; my intention is simply to illustrate the dynamic function of the image where it is found. I am indebted to those who gave permission to use their personal material. Their names and background have been changed to protect their identity.

My conclusions are not to be viewed as a definitive statement regarding the nature of women, for I am considering only one aspect: the instinctive, erotic, dynamic facet of feminine nature. More specifically, I am writing about the positive aspects inherent in the archetypal image of the prostitute. It has two faces, the sacred and the profane. The dark side is readily known; it manifests in the countless mean-spirited ways in which feminine sexuality is misused. The positive aspects are less known, for the sacred elements have been split off.

Stated generally, my purpose is to bring to conscious awareness aspects of feminine nature which have been misunderstood, devalued or lost to the unconscious. In particular, I examine the interrelatedness of sexuality and spirituality and discuss how each may bring life to the other. To this end I demonstrate the manner in which the archetypal image of the sacred prostitute can be an active factor in the lives of modern men and women. Finally, I explore ways to redeem this image from the unconscious, so that the sacred prostitute and what she represents psychologically may have a valued place in contemporary life.

One last observation. In undertaking to write about the sacred prostitute and the goddess, I have chosen figures toward whom many people, women as well as men, may feel some resistance, however unwillingly. Whatever its individual origin, such resistance has a basis I take seriously: the pervasive Logos orientation of our culture. That attitude, to which we are all more or less prone, would have us place a higher value on doing than on being, on achieving rather than experiencing, on thinking more than feeling.

While I respect this view within limits, I have not catered to it here. For instance, I could not present the image of the sacred prostitute by rigorous argumentation or scholarly discourse. My early attempts to do so seemed to take from her the very life I was trying to convey. Like a round peg in a square hole, the image would not fit such a structure. As the reader will see, I have given a place here to imagination and feeling. In this I was guided by my subject. I hope she shows herself in conscientious research, reflective thinking and clear prose—that is, in human narrative for a human audience.

The sacred prostitute, although lost to history in our outer reality, can be a vital, functioning aspect of individual psychic processes. To become conscious of her, to feel her, to allow her expression, adds a new dimension to life—a dimension, as one might imagine, of an erotic and exhilarating nature. It is this sacred servant of the divine goddess, the goddess of love, whom I now present.

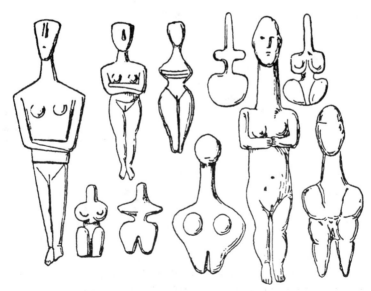

Drawings of stone sculptures of the goddess.
(From Amorgos, Naxos and Crete, pre-Mycenaean, ca. 2000 B.C.)

Inanna-Ishtar, Goddess of Love.
(Stone, Sumerian period)

1

The Goddess and Her Virgin:
Historical Background

O, young damsels, who receive all strangers and give
them hospitality, Priestess of the goddess Pitho in the
rich Corinth, it is you who, in causing the incense to burn
before the image of Venus and in inviting the mother of love,
often merit for us her celestial aid and procure for us the
sweet moments which we taste on the luxurious couches
where is gathered the delicate fruit of beauty.
—B. F. Goldberg, *The Sacred Fire: The Story
of Sex in Religion.*

The Sacred Rituals

Imagine, if you will, traveling to a foreign land, a strange land where
only a few have journeyed. There we come upon the ruins of an ancient civilization, now forgotten. Outlines of half-buried stones suggest the foundation of a once majestic temple. Portions of huge, broken marble columns lay scattered about as if some giant force had
destroyed them.

Wandering among these ruins, imagine the life once lived here.
Our mind's eye can see the temple as it once must have been, glistening in the sunlight, a rectangular structure, spacious, with intri-
cately carved pediments, its roof supported by the massive fluted
columns. Beams of light from all angles penetrate the walls. Through
the open doors we can peer into the inner sanctuary. A figure moves
gracefully before the altar, illuminating it by bringing fire to the clay
oil lamps all around. Behold the priestess of the temple of Venus, the
goddess of love. She is the sacred prostitute.

She is a mystery, concealed by veils. We see her only dimly. Yet
in the flickering light we discern her shapely feminine outline. A
breeze lifts her veils to reveal her long black tresses. Silver bracelets
adorn her arms and ankles; miniature crescents hang from her ear

21

lobes and lapis lazuli beads encircle her neck.[1] Her perfume with its musklike aroma creates an aura which stimulates and enriches physical desire.[2]

As the sacred prostitute moves through the open temple doors she begins to dance to the music of the flute, tambourine and cymbals. Her gestures, her facial expressions and the movements of her supple body all speak to the welcoming of passion. There is no false modesty regarding her body, and as she dances the contours of her feminine form are revealed under an almost transparent saffron robe. Her movements are graceful, as she is well aware of her beauty. She is full of love, and as she dances her passion grows. In her ecstasy she forgets all restraint and gives herself to the deity and to the stranger.

"A thousand pens of gold, and ink scented with musk,"[3] are needed to describe the feminine appeal, beauty and sensuality of this vision as she quickly passes through our mind's eye back into the dark recesses of the temple.

Imagine the sacred prostitute greeting the stranger, a world-weary man who has come to the temple to worship the goddess of love. No words are spoken; her outstretched arms and the soft, warm expression of her radiant eyes and face say what needs to be said. In her private chambers, the sacred love-room of the temple, filled with the fragrance of herbs and flowers, she bathes the stranger, offering him balm. She tells him amusing stories of her training—how the temple priests and other ritual priestesses taught her the art of love-making. "Keep your fingertips close to your knees and your eyes lowered. When you look sideways try to press your chin into your shoulder,"[4] she tells him, playfully mocking them.

She prepares a tray of fresh dates, nuts and fruit which she lays before him, along with bread dipped in honey. The sacred prostitute and the stranger drink sweet wine from a single silver cup. She came to the temple, she tells him, in order to fulfill the law of the land, which every maiden must do. With reverence she speaks of her

---

[1] Such jewelry, dating back to 3000 B.C.E. and found in various Mid-Eastern regions, is commonly seen in museums.

[2] The perfume in these ancient times was derived from the sexual glands of animals. Very small vials made of alabaster and other semiprecious stones used as containers for this costly and treasured substance can also be seen in museums.

[3] O.A. Wall, *Sex and Sex Worship*, p. 243.

[4] James A. Michener, *The Source*, p. 123.

devotion to the goddess as she approaches the small marble image of Venus. In the near darkness, alone in her rapture, she performs the ritual of lighting the perfumed oil lamp, gently swaying and chanting softly in prayer of thanksgiving to the goddess.

The stranger watches quietly and thinks to himself,

> How different she is from me, how strangely different! She is afraid of me, and my male difference. She is getting herself naked and clear of her fear. How sensitive and softly alive she is, with a life so different from mine! How beautiful with a soft strange courage, of life. . . . How terrible to fail her, or to trespass on her![5]

As the sacred prostitute turns back to the stranger she removes her saffron robe and gestures to him to stand before the image of Venus. He moves awkwardly at first, but deep within the stirring of his manhood gives impetus to strong strides. He kneels in honor before the goddess of passion and love, and offers a prayer of supplication that she will receive his offering.

The sacred prostitute leads the stranger to the couch prepared with white linens and aromatic myrtle leaves. She has rubbed sweet smelling wild thyme on her thighs. Her faint smile and glistening eyes tell the stranger that she is full of desire for him. The gentle touch of her embrace sparks a fiery response—he feels the quickening of his body. He is keenly aware of the passion within this votary to the goddess of love and fertility, and is fulfilled.

The woman and the stranger know that the consummation of the love act is consecrated by the deity through which they are renewed. The ritual itself, due to the presence of the divine, is transforming. The sacred prostitute, now no longer a maiden, is initiated into the fullness of womanhood, the beauty of her body and her sexuality. Her true feminine nature is awakened to life. The divine element of love resides in her.

The stranger too is transformed. The qualities of the receptive feminine nature, so opposite from his own, are embedded deep within his soul; the image of the sacred prostitute is viable within him. He is fully aware of the deep emotions within the sanctuary of his heart. He makes no specific claims on the woman herself, but carries her image, the personification of love and sexual joy, into the world. His experience of the mysteries of sex and religion opens the

---

5 D.H. Lawrence, *The Man Who Died,* p. 203.

door to the potential of on-going life; it accompanies the regeneration of the soul.

We are privileged also to witness the most important celebration in this strange land, the feast of the New Year. This festival is unusual for it lasts many days and occurs during the time of the summer solstice, when the land and vegetation are parched and brown from the scorching summer sun.

Great feasts with ample containers of beer and wine are prepared at the temple of love; after all, it is the locus of potency and fertility. The temple musicians play lively music which enhances the merriment, the dancing and love-making. During the celebration, sacrifices are also made in the temple in order to return to the goddess in thanksgiving some portion of the life she has provided. The first grains and fruits, the first offspring of the livestock, and even the first child—that which was most precious—are sacrificed to her. The people of this time and locale feel the connection of blood and fertility. In these rituals they offer up libations of blood to increase the power which gives more abundant life to earth.[6]

Entering into the festivities, we find that the celebration culminates in the *hieros gamos,* the sacred marriage. This ritual is the traditional reenactment of the marriage of the goddess of love and fertility with her lover, the young, virile vegetation god. The chosen sacred prostitute, a special votary who is regarded as the personification of the goddess, unites with the reigning monarch, identified with the god. This union assures productivity of the land and fruitfulness of the womb of both human and beast; it is the "fixing of destinies."[7]

At the beginning, joyous music and ecstatic love songs fill the air, capturing the passionate and erotic musings of the sacred prostitute as she makes her special preparations for this most important observance.

> When for the wild bull, for the lord, I shall have bathed,
> When for the shepherd Dumuzi, I shall have bathed,
> When with . . . my sides I shall have adorned,

---

[6] Today we may find these rites cruel, primitive and pagan, and choose to dismiss them as such. Yet to better comprehend the rationale behind such practices we must view the ritual as enacted in much the same way as, for instance, the Holy Eucharist, which according to Christian tradition is built on a human sacrifice—the symbolic libation of blood for the strengthening of life.

[7] S.H. Hooke, *Babylonian and Assyrian Religion,* p. 54.

When with amber my mouth I shall have coated,
When with kohl my eyes I shall have painted,
Then in his fair hands my loins shall have been shaped,
When the lord, lying by holy Inanna, the shepherd Dumuzi,
With milk and cream the lap shall have smoothed . . . ,
When on my vulva his hands he shall have laid,
When like his black boat, he shall have . . . it,
When like his narrow boat, he shall have brought life to it,
When on the bed he shall have caressed me,
Then shall I caress my lord, a sweet fate I shall decree for him,
I shall caress Shulgi, the faithful shepherd, a sweet fate I
    shall decree for him,
I shall caress his loins, the shepherdship of all the lands,
I shall decree as his fate.[8]

After much feasting and merriment, the bridal couple retires to the sacred chambers of the ziggurat, the tower of the temple. There the nuptial bed is perfumed with myrrh, aloes and cinnamon. The waiting masses sing hymns and love songs to enhance the rapture and the fertilizing power of the goddess and her lover, the sacred prostitute and the king.

The king goes with lifted head to the holy lap,
He goes with lifted head to the holy lap of Inanna,
The king coming with lifted head,
Coming to my queen with lifted head . . .
Embraces the Hierodule . . .[9]

What would we feel standing at the foot of the ziggurat? If we were fortunate, we would be filled with awe so that our experience would be a kind of participation. Perhaps we could share the feelings

---

[8] Samuel Kramer, *The Sacred Marriage Rite,* p. 63. This text is translated from the Gudea Cylinders (ca. 3000 B.C.E.) of ancient Sumer. The poetry is written about Inanna, perhaps the oldest of the goddesses of passion, love and death. Dumuzi was the shepherd king of Erech who came to be known as the first ruler to wed Inanna in the sacred marriage rite. Literally the name means "faithful son." The lacunae in the text indicate portions where the clay tablets have been destroyed or are nontranslatable.

[9] Ibid., p. 83. The term hierodule is commonly used in descriptions of the sacred prostitute. Literally it means "sacred servant." It is employed by scholars to designate religious officials whose functions included sexual rites. The word stems from the Greek root *hieros,* meaning sacred or holy, and that word, in turn, is related to an earlier form, *eis,* for "words denoting passion." (American Heritage Dictionary)

of the sacred prostitute whose human desires and emotions, and creative chthonic energies, are expressions of the divine. Perhaps we could share in her understanding that the nature of the goddess dwells within her feminine being.

The Priestess

The sacred prostitute, whom we have beheld here in imagination, was a reality of ancient times. Inscribed clay tablets, unearthed relics and excavated temples tell of religious ceremonies celebrating the potent goddesses of love and fertility.[10] Through recorded laws and ancient documents we know of the existence of women who participated in these sacred rituals. But what do we know about the women themselves? What were the joys or complexities of their everyday lives? And what was their relationship to the goddess?

Writings from the ancient civilization of Sumer shed some light on these questions. There the goddess of love in her celestial beauty was worshiped as the moon goddess. Actually, the first writer in history whose name and works have been preserved was Enheduanna (born ca. 2300 B.C.), a priestess of the moon goddess.[11] Her poetry reads like a personal diary, filled with her adoration of the moon goddess, political upheavals, her banishment from the temple and her return. She writes with sensuality and intimacy to the goddess of love, Inanna. "She speaks to a deity who has descended to earth as an ally, as a friend to help her in her need."[12] She writes of her image of the goddess Inanna and the Divine Essences:

> Lady of all the essences, full of light,
> good woman clothed in radiance
> whom heaven and earth love,
> temple friend of An,
> you wear great ornaments,

---

[10] Though for the most part I refer to "the" goddess, even at times specifically to Venus or Aphrodite, in history many goddesses were worshiped. What I say here applies in general. Other goddesses are mentioned by name in chapter 2 under the subheading, "The Goddess."

[11] See Aliki Barnstone and Willis Barnstone, eds., *A Book of Women Poets from Antiquity to Now,* p. 1: "Enheduanna was a moon priestess, the daughter of King Sargon of Agade (2334-2279 B.C.) who reigned over the world's first empire, extending from the Mediterranean to Persia."

[12] Ibid.

you desire the tiara of the high priestess
whose hand holds the seven essences.
O my lady, guardian of all the great essences,
you have picked them up and hung them
on your hand.
You have gathered the holy essences
    and worn them
tightly on your breasts.[13]

Enheduanna also experiences the powerful wrath and fury of her
love goddess, the goddess of the moon in her dark phase:

Like a dragon you have filled the land
with venom.
Like thunder when you roar over the earth,
trees and plants fall before you.
You are a flood descending from a mountain,
O primary one,
moon goddess Inanna of heaven and earth!
Your fire blows about and drops on our nation.
Lady mounted on a beast,
An gives you qualities, holy commands,
and you decide.
You are in all our great rites.
Who can understand you?[14]

The moon priestess realizes the absence of love when the goddess
is not present in the lives of the people:

. . . you have lifted your foot and left
their barn of fertility.
The women of the city no longer speak of love
with their husbands.
At night they do not make love.
They are no longer naked before them,
revealing intimate treasures.
Great daughter of Suen,
impetuous wild cow, supreme lady commanding An,
who dares not worship you?[15]

---

13 Ibid., p. 2.

14 Ibid.

15 Ibid., p. 4.

Female figurine
invoking the power of
the moon goddess.
(Terracotta, Egypt,
ca. 4000 B.C.)

Apparently a new ruler, Lugalanne, came to power and changed the sacred rituals. Enheduanna, as high priestess, was banished from the temple. She writes of her despair and the loss of her feminine beauty when she no longer felt the connection to her love goddess:

> You asked me to enter the holy cloister,
> the *giparu,*
> and I went inside, I the high priestess
> Enheduanna!
> I carried the ritual basket and sang
> your praise.
> Now I am banished among the lepers.
> Even I cannot live with you.
> Shadows approach the light of day, the light
> is darkened around me,
> shadows approach the daylight,
> covering the day with sandstorm.
> My soft mouth of honey is suddenly confused.
> My beautiful face is dust.[16]

But then Enheduanna is restored to her former station. She knows once again her joy, her beauty and her relationship to the goddess:

> The first lady of the throne room
> has accepted Enheduanna's song.
> Inanna loves her again.
> The day was good for Enheduanna, for she was dressed
> in jewels.
> She was dressed in womanly beauty.
> Like the moon's first rays over the horizon,
> how luxuriously she was dressed!
> When Nanna, Inanna's father,
> made his entrance
> the palace blessed Inanna's mother Ningal.
> From the doorsill of heaven came the word:
> "Welcome!"[17]

The descriptive and sensitive writings of Enheduanna bring to light the deep devotion of an individual human woman, a priestess, to the love goddess. Enheduanna experiences her beauty and sensuality as gifts bestowed by the goddess. When she can no longer wor-

---

[16] Ibid.
[17] Ibid., p. 8.

ship in the temple, she feels a dark and shadowy emptiness, and her own reflection of the goddess, her radiant feminine beauty, is concealed. When the goddess was banished, intimate pleasures and the language of love could not continue in the lives of the people.

Through the imagery in Enheduanna's poetry and historical accounts of the sacred prostitute, we can more clearly understand her significance in the religious rituals where she was the major and decisive figure. Yet the sacred prostitute remains a mystery, in large part because our modern attitude makes it difficult for us to grasp what we see as a paradox in her image: her sexual nature was an integral aspect of her spiritual nature. For most of us that conjunction is a contradiction. In ancient times, however, it was a unity.

The Origins of Sacred Prostitution

During the millennium when the sacred prostitute existed, cultures were built on a matriarchal system. Matriarchy here does not simply mean that women replaced men in authority positions; rather, the focus was on different cultural values.

> Where patriarchy establishes law, matriarchy establishes custom; where patriarchy establishes military power, matriarchy establishes religious authority; where patriarchy encourages the *aresteia* of the individual warrior, matriarchy encourages the tradition-bound cohesion of the collective.[18]

Matriarchy was concerned with cultural authority as opposed to the political power emphasized by the patriarchy.[19]

In the ancient matriarchies, nature and fertility were the core of existence. The people lived close to nature, therefore their gods and goddesses were nature divinities. Their deities ordered destiny by providing or denying abundance to the earth. Inherent in the individual's human nature was erotic passion. Desire and sexual response experienced as a regenerative power were recognized as a gift or a blessing from the divine. Man's and woman's sexual nature and their religious attitude were inseparable. In their praises of thanksgiving or in their supplications, they offered the sex act to the goddess revered

---

[18] William Thompson, *The Time Falling Bodies Take to Light,* p. 149.

[19] Ibid., p. 150. It should be understood that men are not synonymous with the patriarchy any more than women are solely responsible for a matriarchy. The terms refer to attitudinal differences.

for love and passion. It was an act, honorable and pious, pleasing to both the deity and mortal alike. The practice of sacred prostitution evolved within this matriarchal religious system and thus made no separation between sexuality and spirituality.

There are other speculations on the origins of sacred prostitution. Perhaps it grew, as many customs do, from a simple need. It was primarily women who performed the menial tasks of the sacred places, and in time, as they were associated with sacred things, they acquired a certain sanctity. Being unattached, these women were sought out by men; consequently, their religious powers grew. They were thought to be in close relationship with the gods—often such a woman was considered to be the wife of a male deity. Thus she was endowed with the power to interpret his will or to grant a blessing or a curse.[20]

Another hypothesis regarding the institutionalization of sacred prostitution stems from a civil rite. In early primitive tribes, a young girl was offered to an appointed tribal member, someone other than a man who could be her husband, for a defloration ceremony. It was an initiation rite into tribal membership. As the tribe developed culturally, this act was offered to the tribal god in order to procure divine favor. A vestige of this rite was evident in medieval Europe in the so-called *jus prima noctis* (or *droit de seigneur)*, the right of the lord of the manor to the first night with a bride. He might relinquish this right for a fee or he might insist on the defloration himself. In either case the bride had to present herself to the feudal lord before joining her husband.[21]

Still other writers explain the origins of sacred prostitution as a development of the cult of the Great Mother or Mother Earth. She was the goddess of all fertility, her blessing for reproduction of crops and children and animal life being vital to the early agrarian cultures. Connected to the goddess of fertility, although in a subordinate position, was the son-lover husband. It was supposed that as this union of the goddess and her consort ensured fertility for the land, so it should be imitated by the women who sought her blessing.[22]

---

[20] James G. Frazer, *The Golden Bough: A Study in Magic and Religion,* vol. 1, p. 71.

[21] B.F. Goldberg, *The Sacred Fire: The Story of Sex in Religion,* p. 51.

[22] Frazer, *The Golden Bough,* vol. 1, p. 39.

Whatever the reason or combination of reasons for its development, there is no question that sacred prostitution existed for thousands of years in widespread civilizations. Wherever the goddess of fertility, love and passion was worshiped, the sacred prostitute was an integral member of the community.

An ancient record of the goddess comes from the land of Sumer, often referred to as the cradle of civilization. Clay tablets inscribed in cuneiform—the Gudea Cylinders[23]—tell stories of the goddess Inanna, Queen of Heaven and Earth, The Morning and Evening Star. Inanna, a prominent deity in the Sumerian pantheon, brought to earth in the Boat of Heaven gifts of civilization and culture, such as music, crafts, judgments and truth. She also brought the art of love-making, a cultural achievement. These ancient texts also introduce the sacred prostitute as hierodule.

The following poem describes the goddess as "you who sweeten all things," and confirms the similarity between the goddess and the sacred prostitute:

> The faithful shepherd, he of the sweet chant,
> Will utter a resounding chant for you,
> Lordly Queen, you who sweeten all things,
> Inanna, it will bring joy to your heart.
>
> Lordly Queen, when you enter the stall
> Inanna, the stall rejoices with you,
> Hierodule, when you enter the sheepfold,[24]
> The stall rejoices with you . . .[25]

This many-faceted goddess of love, passion, war and death was called Ishtar by the Babylonians. Her sexual activity was emphasized through descriptions of her as "the sweet voiced mistress of the gods,"[26] yet she was also known for her cruel and relentless fickleness toward her lovers. Since she was the bringer of love and sexual joy, she also held the power to take them away. Without this tempting, full-breasted goddess, nothing that concerned the life cycle could come to pass. When Ishtar makes her descent into the Nether World,

---

[23] See above, note 8.

[24] Diane Wolkstein and Samuel Kramer, *Inanna: Queen of Heaven and Earth,* p. 146: "In Sumerian, the word for sheepfold, womb, vulva, loins, and lap is the same."

[25] Kramer, *Sacred Marriage Rite,* p. 101.

[26] Raphael Patai, *The Hebrew Goddess,* p. 188.

no passion is felt on earth; sterility overcomes the land, in a situation similar to that which the moon priestess, Enheduanna, described. The poets explain:

> Since the Lady Ishtar descended to the land of No-Return
> The bull does not spring upon the cow, the ass does not
>   bow over the jenny
> The man no more bows over the woman in the street,
> The man sleeps in his chamber
> The woman sleeps alone.[27]

Again on her return to earth, life and love are awakened, as Ishtar exclaims in a hymn:

> I turn the male to the female;
> I am she who adorneth the male for the female,
> I am she who adorneth the female for the male.[28]

Ishtar was called the Great Goddess Har, Mother of Harlots. "Her high priestess, the Harine, was considered the spiritual ruler of 'the city of Ishtar.'"[29] An ancient ivory wall carving depicts Ishtar seated in a window frame. In this typical pose of the prostitute, she is known as "Kilili Mushriti," or "Kilili who leans out." She says, "A prostitute compassionate am I."[30]

An account of sacred prostitution is recorded in the Gilgamesh Epic, completed about 7000 B.C.E., though possibly it comes from a much older oral tradition.[31] The story describes the heroic feats of the legendary King Gilgamesh, who was part human and part god. He spurned Ishtar's amorous advances and was so powerful that the deities became angry.

The gods design a plan to rob Gilgamesh of his authority and domination. On the uncultivated plains they place a wild hairy man, Enkidu. So like the animals is he that he roams and grazes with them. Enkidu is spotted by a hunter at the watering hole where the animals come to drink. Gilgamesh is told of this and plans to capture

---

[27] M. Esther Harding, *Woman's Mysteries: Ancient and Modern,* p. 159.

[28] Ibid.

[29] Barbara Walker, *The Woman's Encyclopedia of Myths and Secrets,* p. 820.

[30] Nor Hall, *The Moon and the Virgin ,* p. 11.

[31] See Alexander Heidel, *The Gilgamesh Epic and Old Testament Parallels,* pp. 14f.

the wild, animal man. He sends a *herem,* a sacred prostitute consecrated to the goddess, to the watering place with the hunter.

When they come upon Enkidu the hunter bids the woman remove
her garments, "laying bare her ripeness." She "opened wide her garments, exposing her charms, yielded herself to his embraces, and
for six days and seven nights gratified his desire, until he was won
from his wild life."[32] Alienated now from his animal companions,
Enkidu is led by the sacred prostitute to the gates of the city, the center of human civilization.

Initiation into Womanhood

From these ancient chronicles the image of the sacred prostitute
emerges. In her embodiment of the goddess, she is the bringer of
sexual joy and the vessel by which the raw animal instincts are
transformed into love and love-making. It is in this sense that Hesiod
said, "the sensual magic of the sacred whores or Horae 'mellowed
the behavior of men.'"[33] In later civilizations, the sacred prostitutes

> were often known as Charites or Graces, since they dealt in the
> unique combination of beauty and kindness called *charis* (Latin, *cari-
> tas*) that was later translated 'charity.' Actually it was like Hindu
> *karuna,* a combination of mother-love, tenderness, comfort, mystical
> enlightenment and sex.[34]

We find additional information to enlarge our picture of the sacred
prostitute in the writings of Herodotus, a third-century (B.C.E.)
Greek historian.

> Babylonian custom . . . compels every woman of the land once in
> her life to sit in the temple of love and have intercourse with some
> stranger . . . the men pass and make their choice. It matters not what
> be the sum of money; the woman will never refuse, for that were a
> sin, the money being by this act made sacred. After their intercourse
> she has made herself holy in the sight of the goddess and goes away
> to her home; and thereafter there is no bribe however great that will
> get her. So then the women that are tall and fair are soon free to de-
> part, but the uncomely have long to wait because they cannot fulfill

[32] James Hastings, ed., *Encyclopaedia of Religion and Ethics,* vol. 6, p.
673.

[33] Walker, *Woman's Encyclopedia of Myths and Secrets,* p. 820.

[34] Ibid.

the law; for some of them remain for three years or four. There is a custom like to this in some parts of Cyprus.[35]

Thus before entering marriage each Babylonian maiden was initiated into womanhood within the sanctity of the temple, sacrificing her maidenhood and experiencing the first fruits of her sexuality. The stranger, who was viewed as an emissary of the gods, came and threw coins into the lap of the woman of his choice and said, "May the goddess Mylitta make thee happy,"[36] always recognizing the presence of the deity and the sanctity of the act. He did not pay for the woman, but gave to the goddess for allowing him to partake of her sacrificial rite. Both the act of love-making and the offering were dedicated and thus made holy. The woman then returned to her home, usually to prepare for her forthcoming marriage. She was now blessed. No disgrace, but rather honor, was accorded her for this act.

It was an honor which in some countries only the highest-born could achieve, and they did so throughout continuing generations. Strabo declares that

> a very beautiful virgin of most distinguished lineage was consecrated to Zeus (Amon), and . . . played the concubine and had intercourse with whomsoever she desired until the natural purification of her body was accomplished (i.e., until the expiration of a month); then, after her purification, she was given to a husband.[37]

In Thebes the wife of the high priest was entitled "chief concubine," while the queen or princess was often called the "wife of the god." Herodotus writes that a bed on which the wife of the god slept for his enjoyment was placed in the inner sanctuary of the ziggurat where the god would come to claim his wife. When speaking of her parentage, the famous Queen Hatshepsut, of the XVIII dynasty, claims the god Amon had intercourse with her mother.[38]

> When it was thought that a god could thus treat women—and women, too, who had earthly husbands—it is probable that, under religious regulation, provision was made for similar conduct on the part of his worshippers.[39]

---

[35] Quoted in Harding, *Woman's Mysteries,* p. 159.

[36] Goldberg, *The Sacred Fire,* p. 78.

[37] Hastings, *Encyclopaedia of Religion and Ethics,* vol. 6, p. 675.

[38] Ibid., p. 676.

[39] Ibid.

Roman matrons of the highest aristocracy came to the temple of Juno Sospita to enter into the act of sacred prostitution when a revelation was needed.[40]

In Egypt the goddesses Hathor and Bastet were worshiped as fertility goddesses. Often they are pictured nude, accompanied by a chorus of dancing women. In their great festival times, "temporary hierodules went in large numbers . . . playing and singing. . . . In the light of the Goddesses' character, the nature of the services of these women is not difficult to divine."[41]

After these occasions of great celebration, the women did not remain in service of the deity. Having fulfilled their obligation on the night of the ritual, they returned home to resume their daily lives. At Hierapolis in Lebanon, the modern Baalbek, "matrons as well as maids prostituted themselves in the service of the goddess, Attar."[42] "Women prostituted themselves, and virgins forthwith vowed their virginity to prostitution."[43] There, it appeared that a tradition of both matron and maiden, temporary and permanent votary to the goddess, was established.

In some instances, women not wishing to lead a chaste life or to enter into marriage spent their entire lives in the temple compounds. Such were the Vestal Virgins, who did not unite with a husband but became the "bride" in a ritual marriage with the king as the surrogate for a god. They served the goddess of Greece and Rome, Hestia or Vesta, in tending to the hearth fires. The hearth was "the omphalos, feminine hub of the universe, navel-stone of the temple."[44] Their feminine nature "was dedicated to a higher purpose, that of bringing the fertilizing power of the goddess into effective contact with the lives of human beings."[45]

In other cases the woman's path to sacred prostitution came about through subjection to a warring victor. Ramses III attests to this in his inscription detailing captives taken in the Syrian War. "I have carried them away: the males to fill thy storehouse, their women, to

---

[40] Walker, *Woman's Encyclopedia of Myths and Secrets*, p. 820.

[41] Hastings, *Encyclopaedia of Religion and Ethics*, vol. 6, p. 676.

[42] Ibid., p. 674.

[43] Ibid.

[44] Walker, *Woman's Encyclopedia of Myths and Secrets*, p. 821.

[45] Harding, *Woman's Mysteries*, p. 132.

be subjects of thy temple."[46] The beautiful scenes pictured on the wall of the temple erected by Ramses confirm the presence of the women and their act of love-making.[47]

However they came to the temple of love, by law, dedication or servitude, of royal or common birth, for a night or a lifetime, we know that the sacred prostitutes were many in number. According to Strabo, at the temples of Aphrodite in Eryx and Corinth there were above a thousand, while at each of the two Comanas about six thousand were in residence.[48] They were accorded social status and were educated. In some cases, they remained politically and legally equal to men.

In the code of Hammurabi, special legislation protected the rights and good name of the sacred prostitute; she was protected from slander, as were her children, by the same law which upheld a married woman's reputation. Also by law, the sacred prostitute could inherit property from her father and receive income from the land worked by her brothers. If dissatisfied she could dispose of the property in ways which she saw fit. Considering the role of women at the time, this was an extraordinary right.

There were special houses where sacred prostitutes usually lived, although residence was not compulsory. If a woman chose to live outside the provided housing arrangement, she was prohibited on pain of death from opening a wine shop. Perhaps it was thought that such an establishment would be too similar to the taverns inhabited by the profane prostitute, who also existed in large numbers at the same times and in the same places.

Profane Prostitution

Although there were certain restrictions on the lives of sacred prostitutes, for the most part they enjoyed greater privileges than women in common life.[49] Profane prostitutes, however, had a difficult life.[50]

---

[46] Hastings, *Encyclopaedia of Religion and Ethics,* vol. 6, p. 675.

[47] Ibid.

[48] Ibid., p. 672. There were male sacred prostitutes as well, called *qadhesh,* emasculated priests who dressed in women's clothing and fulfilled the woman's function.

[49] Ibid., p. 673.

[50] William W. Sanger, M.D., *History of Prostitution,* p. 77. The material regarding prostitution in ancient times is covered in pages 35-75.

For millenniums profane prostitution was prevalent, as were brothels, taverns and places of entertainment. When Pompeii was excavated, some houses were found with the ithyphallic symbol above the doorway and inside small cells with sensuous wall paintings; these were thought to be the places where "slave girls of the bawd" enticed men who sought sexual entertainment.

During Trajan's reign, in Rome alone thirty-two thousand prostitutes were registered in the office of the aedile, as required by law; however, it was reasoned that their actual number was much higher. They were subject to abuse, arrest and banishment from the city.

The profane prostitute was not allowed to ride in any vehicle, and by law her dress was prescribed to distinguish her from other women. In Rome she wore a toga as did men, while in Greece her clothes were of a flowery material. She was not allowed to wear the rich purples, fine cloth, shoes or jewelry which were the mark of a woman of repute. Usually her hair was dyed yellow or red and, in Greece, even blue. The profane prostitute was not allowed to mix with society and was often not allowed on the streets in the daytime. It was forbidden for her to enter the temples or to participate in any religious ceremony.

According to the regulations set down by Solon in Greece, the profane prostitute forfeited rights of citizenship, and her children were considered bastards. The children could not acquire citizenship except by performing some special act of heroism. In Athens, the *Dicteriades,* as the prostitutes were called, were often bought with public money and placed in state-owned brothels, their meager earnings going into state coffers. A privileged few were the beautiful courtesans of wealthy men, and they were protected from the law. Although very much in the minority, these *hetairae,* as they were known, were famous for their charm, intellect and influence on the men who supported them in stylish and extravagant ways. Yet they were not free.

In Rome it was common for women, even young girls, to be sent into prostitution as punishment for crime.

> When a bawd had purchased a virgin as a slave, or when, as sometimes happened under the later emperors, a virgin was handed to him to be prostituted as a punishment for crime, the door of his house was adorned with twigs of laurel; a lamp of unusual size was hung out at night, and a tablet . . . stated that a virgin had been received, . . . enumerating her charms with cruel grossness. When a purchaser had been found and a bargain struck, the unfortunate girl, often a

mere child, was surrendered to his brutality, and the wretch issued from the cell afterward, to be himself crowned with laurel by the slaves of the establishment.[51]

Prostitution outside the precincts of the temple was thus apparently a cruel and brutalizing sport. The degradation of the profane prostitute—who represents the dark side of feminine sexuality—was profound; she was the very antithesis of the sacred prostitute, whose sexuality revered the goddess; yet they existed in juxtaposition. One wonders what led some women and men to the temple of love and others to the brothel.

The Sacred Marriage

In the temple of love the sacred prostitute's primary offering to the goddess was her welcoming of the stranger, thought to be the emissary of the gods or perhaps the god incarnate. If she were a maiden, he initiated her into the mysteries of her feminine sexuality under the aegis of the goddess.

Since the stranger was someone other than the man she would marry, she could participate without reservations or concerns about security or social acceptance. With the stranger she was awakened to her innate feminine nature of giving, receiving and containing love. To him the sacred prostitute offered a rekindling of the divine spark of life, a full and complete sense of well-being, perhaps sorely lacking in the world outside the sacred precincts. Intercourse with her was a regeneration through the mystery of sex, which paralleled the mystery of religious teachings. The flesh and the spirit were united, each supporting the other.

The sacred prostitute was a primary participant in the new moon festivals and other religious ceremonies. Her dancing provoked much merriment and desire for love-making. With the other celebrants, she feasted on little moon cakes[52] and copious amounts of beer and wine. She could readily enter into this Dionysian splendor.

In the most important ritual, that of the *hieros gamos,* the sacred prostitute was the votary chosen to embody the goddess. She was the goddess' fertile womb, her passion and her erotic nature. In the

---

[51] Ibid.

[52] Numerous little crescent-shaped clay molds used for baking have been found at excavation sites.

union with the god, embodied by the reigning monarch, she assured the fertility and well-being of the land and the people.[53]

Whether in public celebration or in the quiet privacy of her temple chamber, the sacred prostitute expressed her true feminine nature. Her beauty and sensuous body were not used in order to gain security, power or possessions. She did not make love in order to obtain admiration or devotion from the man who came to her, for often she remained veiled and anonymous. She did not require a man to give her a sense of her own identity; rather this was rooted in her own womanliness. The laws of her feminine nature were harmonious with those of the goddess.[54] Her raison d'être was to worship the goddess in love-making, thereby bringing the goddess' love into the human sphere.

In this union—the union of masculine and feminine, spiritual and physical—the personal was transcended and the divine entered in. As the embodiment of the goddess in the mystical union of the sacred marriage, the sacred prostitute aroused the male and was the receptacle for his passion. Her human emotions and her creative, bodily energies were united with the suprapersonal. She touched basic regenerative powers, and thereby, as the goddess incarnate, assured the continuity of life and love. The sacred prostitute was the holy vessel wherein chthonic and spiritual forces united.

The Demise of Sacred Prostitution

Moving in giants steps through subsequent historical and cultural patterns, we find the image of the sacred prostitute drastically altered. There came a time when the goddess was no longer worshiped; then the physical and spiritual aspects of the feminine were declared evil. As crucial as the life of the sacred prostitute is to a full understanding of feminine nature, we must also address the attitudes surrounding her demise, since both are relevant to a clear picture of modern feminine psychology.

When the sacred prostitute was no longer a vital, functioning aspect of the lives of men and women, what were the consequences?

---

[53] For a more complete description of these rituals, see Harding, *Woman's Mysteries,* chapters 10 and 11, "Priests and Priestesses of the Moon" and "The Sacred Marriage."

[54] Ibid., p. 132.

Through the ages, the prevailing matriarchal and matrilineal system evolved into one that was patriarchal and patrilineal. As archaic societies changed from being a contained environment, where agriculture and religion were the primary nucleus of life, to one where commerce, war and expansion became the focus, the prevailing patterns crumbled and new structures emerged. Causes for this gradual shift from matriarchy to patriarchy have been investigated by numerous historians; although this topic is far too extensive and complex to be developed here, some concepts must be put in context because they relate to the change in attitudes toward the feminine.

Existential philosophy suggests that woman's duties in her early world were restricted by her biological make-up. She did not know the pride of creation; birth and suckling were natural functions and not activities. She perpetuated life and maintained life, but it was the same life. Man's design was not to repeat himself in time; in his creativity, he burst out of the present into the future. His existence was one of activity, of exploration, of leaping boundaries or remodeling life as it existed. His feats were celebrated in great festivals. Thus a greater importance was placed on the risking of life than on producing life.[55]

Other theories suggest that woman was seen as mysterious, and taboos that surrounded sacred things also surrounded her. Her tie to earth and the procreation of crops and children were gifts from the gods. Man made of her an object of worship. On earth she had no power; it was beyond the human realm that her powers were affirmed. Being outside that realm, she was never viewed by men as a fellow creature.[56] Thus on the one hand she was elevated, while on the other she was subjugated.

Another explanation for the shift is that when man began to perceive his necessary part in procreation, he misunderstood it. He believed that only the male created the new life, which the mother then nourished in her body; therefore this new life was only of his lineage. The authority and rights of the father were absolute and unshared.[57] In this way, patrilineal descent replaced matrilineal, and the male began to make laws according to his new beliefs.

---

[55] See Simone de Beauvoir, *The Second Sex*, p. 63.

[56] Ibid., p. 69.

[57] Ibid., p. 79.

There is surely no one reason for the shift in values; no doubt it resulted from a combination of causes. The triumph of the patriarchate was neither a matter of chance nor the result of a violent revolution.

> The devaluation of woman represents a necessary stage in the history of humanity, for it is not upon her positive value but upon man's weakness that her prestige is founded. In woman are incarnated the disturbing mysteries of nature, and man escapes her hold when he frees himself from nature.[58]

His "escape" enabled man to gain self-awareness and mastery over both his surroundings and himself.[59]

The emergence of politics, militarism and commerce created social stratification. Woman became subordinate because her roles were no longer important to the new values. As trade routes developed and warring tribes conquered other pockets of civilization, the cultures of different peoples began to intermingle. The divinities of one culture were incorporated with those of another. The number of gods and goddesses to be honored escalated into impossible proportions and a new problem arose: what if one should be forgotten? Thus a Supreme God came to be recognized.[60] From the point of view of the dominant patriarchal society, He was a masculine being. Man created God in his image. Man established new religious doctrine and canons according to his belief in masculine supremacy.[61]

Over time, the temples of love gave way to the house of the Lord, radically displacing woman's role in religious rites. In the worship of the goddess, as we have seen, sex was brought openly and with reverence to the very altar of the goddess. In her temple, men and

---

[58] Ibid., p. 75.

[59] When viewing man's collective cultural development psychologically, there appear to be parallels to the individuation process (at least in men). Man must free himself from the forces of the unconscious realm, the chaos of the world of the Great Mother, in order to develop an ego. With a sense of masculine self-identity he can then realize his contrasexual side, the anima. The individuation process brings one into a more complete relationship with feminine nature, both in inner and outer reality.

[60] Abba Eban, *Heritage: Civilization of the Jews,* p. 11.

[61] De Beauvoir, *The Second Sex,* p. 87: "'Men make the gods: women worship them,' as Frazer has said; men indeed decide whether their supreme divinities shall be females or males; woman's place in society is always that which men assign to her; at no time has she ever imposed her own law."

women came to find life and all that it had to offer in sensual pleasure and delight. But with the change in cultural values and the institutionalization of monotheism and patriarchy, the individual came to the house of the Lord to prepare for death, with the promise of eternal happiness if one could but fulfill the laws.

Under the new tradition, woman became Eve, the embodiment of sensuous seduction, the reason for man's downfall; she was tempted by evil forces and in turn she tempted man. Her very existence was a reminder of physical desires, which had to be resisted through fear of eternal punishment. Profane prostitution continued to flourish, and woman's sexual nature was associated with it or judged by it. No longer seen as a gift of the divine, woman's sensuality was debased and exploited. The very qualities for which woman once had been considered sacred now became the reason for which she was degraded.

In the name of the Lord, man set out to destroy all vestiges of the goddess and her advocacy of sexual joy. Love had become dissociated from the body in order for human beings to reach a purely spiritual union with God. Early fathers of the Christian Church, in order not to compromise the security of a masculine, monotheistic religion, strongly repressed any association with the goddess in Church doctrines. The Trinity was of the patriarchate; Mary may be adored but not worshiped, lest she become a channel by which goddess worship might be reestablished. Epiphanius ordered: "Let the Father, the Son and the Holy Spirit be worshiped, but let no one worship Mary."[62] No longer was there an image of the divine feminine. No longer was the feminine envisioned as the source of physical delight and spiritual ecstasy—an overall feeling of inner harmony.

St. Paul spoke on many occasions of the evils of sex and the subordinate position of women. He exhorted his listeners: "It is good for a man not to touch a woman. Nevertheless to avoid fornication, let every man have his own wife."[63] Celibacy was the ideal state but marriage was permitted if the flesh was too weak. "But if they have not contingency, let them marry, for it is better to marry than to burn."[64] With marriage went injunctions also; it was not to be en-

---

[62] Walker, *The Woman's Encyclopedia of Myths and Secrets,* p. 603.

[63] 1 Corinthians 7:1-2. (All Bible references are to the Authorized King James Version).

[64] Ibid., 7:9.

Michelangelo, *The Fall* (detail), Sistine Chapel ceiling, 1508-12.
("The identification of Eve with evil became so natural in Christian
thought that the serpent acquired female features."—Marina Warner,
Alone of all Her Sex.)

tered into for sexual pleasure, but for the purpose of creating new souls to worship God. Not for their own spiritual longing were men and women to cross the threshold of love and love-making. Adhering to canonical law meant that sexual intercourse was only for the purpose of procreation.[65]

The greatest merit, then, was to deny human nature and to abstain from those things that were most pleasant. Since the most cherished joy was sexual congress, ascetic men swore off it altogether and subdued desire by fasting, self-castigation and personal deprivation of all kinds. St. Francis of Assisi ordered a fellow brother to drag him through the streets in order to mortify his body. Still others contrived all imaginable devices to afflict themselves with physical pain and anguish in their attempts to subjugate the body and attain a state of pure spirituality. If these measures did not succeed in deadening all desire, then at times castration was performed.[66]

With the change in religious beliefs and the new attitude toward women, there came major changes in laws concerning women, focused on their economic and sexual activities. No longer were women considered individuals in their own right, free to inherit property and pass it on to their children, as once the laws had protected the sacred prostitute. Women were clearly viewed as a possession of the father and later, often when sold, a possession of the husband. Roman law placed a woman under guardianship and stated that she was imbecilic. In Greece the laws of Solon gave her no rights at all.[67] Hebrew law condemned a woman to death if she was not chaste at the time of marriage, and if she committed adultery she was stoned to death.[68]

A husband could take several wives but a woman's virtue, indeed her very identity, depended on being married and faithful to her husband.[69] "Likewise, ye wives, be in subjection to your own hus-

---

[65] As late as 1976, the Vatican, in its "Declarations on Certain Questions Concerning Ethics," stated that "the deliberate use of the sexual faculty outside normal conjugal relations essentially contradicts the finality of this faculty."

[66] Wall, *Sex and Sex Worship,* pp. 402f.

[67] De Beauvoir, *The Second Sex,* p. 80.

[68] Deuteronomy 22:20.

[69] Merlin Stone, *When God Was a Woman,* p. 190.

bands."[70] The laws of the Manu state, "A woman assumes through legitimate marriage the very qualities of her husband like a river that loses itself in the ocean."[71] Similar attitudes appear in the Koran. "Men have authority over women because God has made the one superior to the other and because they spend their wealth to maintain them. So good women are obedient, guarding the unseen parts as God has guarded them."[72]

Even in the highly civilized Greek culture, the same attitudes existed, as succinctly expressed by the learned Pythagoras: "There is a good principle, which has created order, light and man; and a bad principle, which has created chaos, darkness and woman."[73] These new laws or religious pronouncements express the very antithesis of the attitudes toward women and their sexual nature that were prevalent during the ages when the goddess was worshiped.

The Disembodied Goddess

In this upheaval of evolution, what did happen to the goddess? What became of her archetypal image?

Marie-Louise von Franz explains in her comments on Apuleius' *The Golden Ass* that the goddess

> was given the title of Theotokos and Sophia and played a certain role in the eastern Church, but in the western Catholic Church—*cum grano salis*—she disappeared. . . . In the western Church she was replaced by the institution of the Church. . . . [She was] transformed into the Ecclesia, the Mother Church.[74]

Although the Church maintained that sense of mystery which surrounded the goddess, the warmth and principle of relatedness was replaced by organization, its laws and hierarchies.

According to von Franz, two aspects were lost:

---

[70] 1 Peter 3:1.

[71] De Beauvoir, *The Second Sex,* p. 80.

[72] Merlin Stone, *When God Was a Woman,* p. 195, quoted from The Koran, Sura 4:31. In the chapter, "And the Men of the City Shall Stone Her with Stones," the author elaborates civil and religious laws of the patriarchy.

[73] De Beauvoir, *The Second Sex,* p. 80.

[74] *A Psychological Interpretation of the Golden Ass of Apuleius,* chap. XI, pp. 14-15.

1) the human shape [feminine image] of the goddess, for the institution is not human, and 2) the relationship to matter. [The goddess] was also simply cosmic matter, and this aspect is also not in the institution of the Church.[75]

The Church recognized neither the attributes of the goddess nor the inherent sexual nature of women (or men); consequently, a chasm between body and spirituality was maintained in religious teachings.

Positive qualities of the goddess have been integrated, to some degree, into the figure of the Virgin Mary, particularly in Catholic countries.[76] In predominantly Protestant countries this integration has not transpired, and Mary is eliminated from religious life except as the adoring mother in the Christmas crèche.

Especially during the Middle Ages, worship derived from the goddess reappeared in the form of the cult of the Virgin Mary. In the devotions of the people, particularly in Southern Europe, she was honored above the male Trinity to the extent that Albertus Magnus called her the Great Goddess.[77] Attributed to the Virgin were more miracles than all the saintly beings had performed, mainly miracles of a healing nature or those dealing with problems related to love or fertility. Again, the veneration of the Virgin manifested in a higher status for women and a more positive attitude toward feminine nature.[78] It was the time of courtly love when knighthood was in flower. Sexual love was given the sanction of cultivated taste and aristocratic privilege.

Contrary to Christian morality, courtly love extolled extraconjugal love; women, married or unmarried, were honored by the knight's service, and as his reward the knight had the right to claim his lady, someone other than his wife, in love's act.[79] He, like the stranger,

---

[75] Ibid., p. 15.

[76] Ibid. The psychological significance of the Virgin Mary is discussed below in chapter 5.

[77] Robert Briffault, *The Mothers: A Study of the Origins of Sentiments and Institutions,* vol. 3, p. 499.

[78] Ibid. Briffault quotes the writer A. Rossler: "Respect for women rises and falls with the veneration of the Virgin Mother of God."

[79] See de Beauvoir, *The Second Sex,* p. 100: "Knightly love has often been regarded as platonic; but the truth is that the feudal husband was guardian and tyrant, and the wife sought an extramarital lover; knightly love was a compensation for the barbarism of the official mores. . . . Love, in the

was bringing his offering to the feminine under the inspiration of love. Nor was he to be denied, for according to the principles of chivalry there were canons to which this passion was expected to conform. As in the time of goddess worship, love and passion were not restricted to marriage; the sentiments appropriate to courtly love were quite separate from those appropriate to marriage.[80]

As before, a transformation in the concept of love was to occur as the voice of the Church rose once again. The manners and morals of courtly love were condemned as Christian legislation became more fully established. This transition is most evident in the ballads of the time, which formerly had glorified the feminine being and honored it in the act of love. The later lyric poetry sings the praises of the Virgin: "His lady 'is crowned in heaven and is his hope of Paradise, and the thought of her is all holiness'."[81] Love became so ethereal that no suspicion of sensuality could be associated with it. Once again the recognition of body and nature, that which was once associated with the sacred prostitute, disappeared, and rationality stiffened.

Through the succeeding ages of the Renaissance and the Reformation, the repression of feminine nature became more severe. The positive attributes of the goddess were spiritualized and accorded to the most Holy Virgin. Great cathedrals reaching upward, moving the eye toward heaven, were built in her name. Such attitudes were compensated by negative attitudes toward the earth-bound woman. She was viewed as destructive, in league with the devil, or proclaimed a witch.

This conception of woman was evident in the great witch hunts so prevalent from the fifteenth to the seventeenth centuries. Women who met in secret often indulged in dance or "pagan" rituals that were similar to the worship of the goddess. Skilled in brewing medicine and practicing the healing arts, they became suspect to the rational mind. Those women who protested Church and state controls, and often even those who seemed a bit unusual for one reason or another, were tried for the practice of witchcraft. An estimated six to nine mil-

---

modern sense of the word, appeared in antiquity only outside the bounds of official society."

[80] Briffault, *The Mothers*, p. 428: "Explicitly it is stated on the authority of the Countess of Narbonne that conjugal affection and the true love between lovers are two absolutely different things which . . . have their source in wholly different sentiments."

[81] Ibid., p. 495.

lion people were executed during this time, eighty-five percent of them women.[82]

Now the split in attitudes toward feminine nature began to widen even more. On the one hand, the feminine was untouchable because it was elevated to the extreme heavenly heights; on the other it was debased as wicked and vile. The image of the sacred prostitute, simultaneously deeply spiritual and joyfully sexual, was completely unviable.

In the eras of Puritanism and the Victorian age, collective attitudes toward women and sexuality, especially in the more Protestant countries, are well known. It is these very attitudes, pervasive in the theories of Freudian psychology, which today still wield tremendous influence on concepts of feminine nature and sexuality.[83] Freudian thought, while revolutionary in bringing sexuality to a more conscious realm, was influenced by the prevailing patriarchal concepts. Freud and his early followers did not see beyond their own masculine nature and Victorian attitudes toward women. He accepted the prevalent belief that women were inherently limited.[84]

One must acknowledge Freud's overall importance, but it must also be realized that his writings—as well as those of virtually all early proponents of depth psychology—are based on a man's understanding of female sexuality. From this psychological bias have come the teachings and prevalent viewpoints held by modern men about women. Until recently, even most women have not questioned these views. Such notions are no less an obstacle to the development of true feminine sexuality than the previously mentioned civil laws and religious tenets of the patriarchate.

Two of Freud's most basic hypotheses are the concepts of the castration complex and penis envy. Both are postulated on the assumption that something is the matter with the female genitalia in comparison with that of the male. Freud writes in "The Psychology of Women":

---

[82] Judy Chicago, *The Dinner Party: A Symbol of our Heritage,* p. 160.

[83] A comic yet distressful example of the frustration fostered in women by modern psychology appears in Woody Allen's film *Manhattan,* where two women are overheard at a cocktail party. One says to the other, "When I finally had an orgasm, my psychiatrist said it was the wrong kind."

[84] See Freud, "Some Psychical Consequences of the Anatomical Distinction between the Sexes."

In the boy the castration-complex is formed after he has learnt from the sight of the female genitals that the sexual organ which he prizes so highly is not a necessary part of every human body . . . and thenceforward he comes under the influence of *castration-anxiety,* which supplies the strongest motive force for his further development. The castration complex in the girl, as well, is started by the sight of the genital organs of the other sex. She immediately notices the difference, and it must be admitted its significance. She feels herself at a great disadvantage, and often declares that she would 'like to have something like that too', and falls a victim to *penis-envy,* which leaves ineradicable traces on her development and the character formation, and even in the most favorable instances, is not overcome without a great expenditure of mental energy.[85]

As this passage indicates, Freud based his theories of feminine sexuality on a male model, and assumed that a woman feels as though she were a mutilated man. But there is no reason to assume that masculine pride in the penis necessarily implies a corresponding humiliation for the female.[86] Penis envy does exist, but only where a woman has been unable to accept her unique way of experiencing her sexual nature and remains dependent on a male's view.

Many modern men and women consciously reject such attitudes. Yet these traditional religious and psychological beliefs continue to have a powerful unconscious influence, shaping our attitudes toward the body, our sexual identities and our relationship to the divine. Repressing what was for centuries represented by the sacred prostitute gives rise to frustration, dissatisfaction and neurosis. This is a problem for men as well as women, for if the male's conscious or unconscious attitude toward the feminine is that of superiority or disdain, then the relationship with his anima, his inner feminine nature, as well as with real women in the outer world, is seriously jeopardized.

*

We have seen ancient images of the sacred prostitute, who embodied both the sexuality and spirituality of feminine nature. We have

---

[85] Freud, "The Psychology of Women," in *New Introductory Lectures on Psychoanalysis,* p. 170.

[86] De Beauvoir, *The Second Sex,* p. 43: "In woman the inferiority complex takes the form of a shamed rejection of her femininity. It is not the lack of the penis that causes this complex, but rather woman's total situation."

also seen subsequent cultural developments. Through the ages the pendulum has swung from a matriarchal to a patriarchal social structure; from goddess worship or pantheism to the worship of one Supreme God; from a morality based on the supremacy of body or matter to a morality based on the supremacy of spirituality. Rationality came to predominate over feeling and the nonlinear, creative force of nature. With these developments, humanity was led to new principles and restraints.

History has bequeathed to us profound cultural, social and technical advances, but at the expense of neglecting other aspects equally valuable to the individual's development and sense of well-being. As the masculine spiritual principle became more dominant, the appreciation of feminine instinctual nature receded into the unconscious. It is this nature, so identified with the image of the sacred prostitute, which needs to be redeemed, for it is vital in the movement toward wholeness of men and women alike.

An understanding of the sacred prostitute, the human woman who embodied the qualities of the goddess of love, can enable us to know and respect these qualities in ourselves. Cultural manifestations of change are dependent on widespread psychological modifications in the conscious attitudes of individuals. Thus, if we are to reconnect to the full-bodied goddess of love, the revisioning and renewal of feminine nature is essentially an individual task. This is the direction pursued in the following chapters.

The Great Goddess.
(Stone, ca. 2000 B.C.; Rietberg Museum, Zurich)

2

The Psychological Significance of
Sacred Prostitution

> It has always been the prime function of mythology and rite
> to supply the symbols that carry the human spirit forward,
> in counteraction to those other constant human fantasies
> that tend to tie it back.
> —Joseph Campbell, *The Hero with a Thousand Faces.*

Introduction

When we speak of the sacred prostitute, the stranger who comes to
the temple of the goddess of love, or of the goddess herself, one may
wonder what meaning these figures and the mythological material
associated with them can hold for contemporary men and women.

Ordinarily we think of myths as traditional stories serving to explain phenomena of nature or religious beliefs. But we can also see
myths as describing or explaining the phenomenological nature of the
psyche itself.

Joseph Campbell, for instance, states that myths tell us in symbolic language about "powers of the psyche to be recognized and
integrated in our lives, powers that have been common to the human
spirit forever, and which represent that wisdom of the species by
which man has weathered the millenniums."[1]

Jung said that myths are first and foremost psychic phenomena
which reveal the nature of the soul:

All the mythologized processes of nature, such as summer and winter, the phases of the moon, the rainy seasons, and so forth, are in
no sense allegories [i.e., a paraphrase of conscious contents] of these
objective occurrences; rather they are symbolic expressions of the
inner, unconscious drama of the psyche which becomes accessible to

---

[1] *Myths to Live By,* p. 13.

man's consciousness by way of projection—that is, mirrored in the events of nature.[2]

Myths are to a collective culture what dreams are to the individual. From the symbolism of both myths and dreams we discern psychic events. Thus we find that myths are not just delightful yet idle stories of gods and goddesses, heroes or demons, from a forgotten time; they speak of living psychological material and act as a repository of truths appropriate to an individual's inner life, as well as to the life of the community.

Jung referred to the deeper strata of the psyche as the collective unconscious (or objective psyche), distinguishing it from the personal unconscious. The latter contains psychic material unique to an individual, while the collective unconscious contains psychic components that are omnipresent, unchanging and common to everyone. These unconscious qualities are not individually acquired, but are inherited substrates of the psyche per se (just as instincts are). At these deep "layers" of the psyche, individual uniqueness gives way to autonomous functions, fields of psychic energy, which become increasingly collective; that is, they are inherent in humankind throughout history. Jung called this kind of psychic energy an archetype.

As psychic energy the archetypes have the ability to regulate, modify and color one's experience of oneself and the world; hence they may be thought of as patterns of behavior. Jung writes:

> What we mean by "archetype" is in itself irrepresentable but has effects which make visualizations of it possible, namely, the archetypal images and ideas. We meet with a similar situation in physics: there the smallest particles are themselves irrepresentable but have effects from the nature of which we can build up a model. The archetypal image, the motif or mythologem, is a construction of this kind.[3]

Myths and dreams are born from this layer of the unconscious. They produce symbols whose form and movement tell a story which reveals a psychic element or attribute of an individual or culture.

We find archetypal motifs occurring in myths from all ages and locales, just as we find them in dreams the world over. Archetypal

---

[2] "Archetypes of the Collective Unconscious," *The Archetypes and the Collective Unconscious,* CW 9i, par. 7.

[3] "On the Nature of the Psyche," *The Structure and Dynamics of the Psyche,* CW 8, par. 417.

motifs are products of the unconscious manifesting in consciousness as images or symbols. A symbol is the best possible expression for something essentially unknown.[4] Behind its objective, visible meaning there is an invisible, more profound meaning. The symbol is thus a "nucleus of meaning" and is charged with energy.

As a psychic product, a symbol carries similar energized contents across boundaries of time and space. The universality of the symbol can be seen, for example, in the ubiquitous image of a love goddess. Homer writes of Aphrodite as the smiling goddess, radiant and beautiful. This is identical to the image which Sumerian poets, millenniums before, described as Inanna.

The symbolic image of a love goddess continues to carry a sense of feminine beauty coupled with sensuous desire. Marilyn Monroe, for example, was referred to as a love goddess. She was the outer personification of an inner archetypal image which relates to one aspect of feminine nature. Charged with internal psychic energy, it is projected onto the external world where it finds its reflection in a living form; it may even be projected into an abstract form such as an ideal, something suprahuman, as was the goddess. When we are in love we do feel radiant and beautiful, and we love to laugh.

When the archetype breaks through to consciousness, a characteristic numinous effect is experienced. It is awe-inspiring, bigger than life, and, writes Jung, "may be said in the long run to mould the destinies of individuals by unconsciously influencing their thinking, feeling, and behaviour, even if this influence is not recognized until long afterwards."[5]

Unaware of this inner psychic drama, early man sought an external explanation for the powerful influences on his life, and thus projected onto the gods that which was awesome and mysterious, calling it sacred and surrounding it with special rites. The tales he told to account for inner feelings of exaltation or suffering were not considered personal but were rather objectified and mythologized. Certain expressions in contemporary life are part of the same phenomenon. "The devil made me do it," we say, or, "Lady Luck was with me," or in very fortunate circumstances, "she (or he) was kissed by an angel." Such verbal expressions refer to a pattern of behavior and an archetypal image behind that pattern.

---

[4] "Definitions," *Psychological Types,* CW 5, pars. 814ff.

[5] "The Dual Mother," *Symbols of Transformation,* CW 5, par. 467.

The archetypes at work in one's life reflect a process quite the opposite from "myth making," that is, from experiencing an inner force and projecting it onto something external. One can interpret a myth subjectively, including the images or symbols of which it is comprised, in order to describe the attributes of a particular psychic function within ourselves. We can ask, for instance, What part of me reflects the pattern of the goddess or a devil? In this way myths, like dreams, offer a descriptive road map of unconscious realms on the path of individuation, the movement toward wholeness.

The particular psychic function with which we are here concerned is an aspect of the archetype of the feminine. Ann Ulanov writes that the feminine function in both men and women completes individuation, and is therefore vital to our psychic development:

> This highest phase of confrontation and individuation in both sexes is initiated by the feminine: for the man, through the anima, which leads to the self; for the woman, through the feminine self, not through any contrasexual elements. The feminine, in this sense, is the completing element; it is the feminine which completes the individuation of *each* sex. The masculine initiates the emergence of consciousness from primary unconsciousness; the feminine initiates the completion of consciousness by re-establishing contact with the unconscious.[6]

Ulanov goes on to explain the dual aspects of the feminine function. One aspect is the elementary or static aspect which we relate to the maternal. It is the unchanging and stable factor that fosters feelings of security, protection and acceptance. The other aspect of the feminine is transformative or dynamic:

> The transformative, active side of the feminine principle accents the dynamic elements of the psyche that urge change and transformation. This active side of the feminine is similar to that divine madness of the soul described in Plato's Phaedrus, which invokes primeval forces that take us out of the limitations and conventions of social norms and the reasonable life. Eros in this sense produces ecstasy, a liberation from the conventions of the group. . . . Ecstasy may range from a momentary being taken out of oneself to a profound enlargement of personality.[7]

---

[6] *The Feminine in Jungian Psychology and in Christian Theology,* p. 269.
[7] Ibid., p. 159.

It is this moving, changing, transformative aspect of the feminine that is associated with the goddess of love and with which the sacred prostitute is identified. When it is active, we view the world and ourselves in a different light. Creative juices are stimulated, and rational boundaries or limitations push into the realm of the unconventional and irrational. New attitudes usher in a certain excitement and life itself takes on new meaning. Welcome change proceeds hand-in-hand with creative risk taking. We may also experience these feelings when we are in love, for no matter what their cause, they arise from the transformative aspect of the feminine, that which is related to the goddess of love.

As we have seen, the principle elements in the scenario of sacred prostitution are the goddess, the stranger who comes to the temple, the sacred marriage itself and the sacred prostitute. These archetypal images are still alive in the collective unconscious. They are, in part, the psychic powers which motivate and modify our conscious understanding of ourselves and the world. Emotions, attitudes and ideas arise from this psychic energy. By appreciating the attributes of the goddess, the stranger and the sacred prostitute, and the significance of the sacred marriage, we are able to draw parallels between mythology and psychological material, thereby deepening our understanding of feminine nature in the lives of women and men.

Accordingly, let us explore each element in more detail.

The Goddess

The goddess of love, passion and fertility was known by various names at different times and in different places.

As we have seen, in Sumer she was called Inanna and in Babylonia, Ishtar. The Persians worshiped Anahita while the Caananites, the Hebrews and the Phoenicians went before the altar of Anath, also named Astarte or Ashtart. In Egypt she was named Isis, earlier identified with Hathor. In Lydia, she was identified as Cybele, and the Romans knew her as Venus.

In Greece, she was the beautiful Aphrodite. Aphrodite was not associated with fertility—that was identified with the goddesses Rhea or Demeter. Aphrodite reigned over love and passion, and her image is perhaps the most renowned for these attributes today.

Regardless of her name or locale, the goddess of love is associated with springtime, with nature in bloom, the time when dormant seeds burst forth in splendor. Beauty is the quintessential component; Aphrodite's nakedness is glorified. She is the only goddess to be portrayed nude in classical sculptures. The loveliness of her feminine body is adored and adorned. As Inanna prepared her body with perfumes and cosmetics when anticipating the union with her love, so does Aphrodite, as the Homeric Hymn recounts:

> She went away to Cyprus, and entered her fragrant temple at Paphos, where she has a precinct and a fragrant altar. After going inside she closed the bright doors, and the Graces gave her a bath, they oiled her with sacred olive-oil, the kind that the gods always have on, that pleasant ambrosia that she was perfumed with. Having put on all her beautiful clothing, and having ornamented herself in gold, Aphrodite, lover of laughter, hurried away to Troy, leaving sweet-smelling Cyprus, quickly cutting a path through the clouds high up.[8]

Aphrodite was often referred to as "the golden one." Goldenness not only defines her radiance but also symbolizes a freedom from pollution, as gold is a noncorrosive element. It also denotes consciousness. Carl Kerényi speaks of this consciousness as "something [which is not] heavy or darkly earthy . . . but . . . something bright and lucid."[9] It is the consciousness of relationship and feeling. Bachofen too states that Aphrodite's realm of consciousness is not spiritual but earthly consciousness "exalted to the highest purity."[10]

The goddess exemplifies those aspects of feminine nature which are manifested in matter. Physical beauty, feminine consciousness integrated in the body (i.e., instinctive wisdom) and the interconnecting capacity for deep-felt emotions and relatedness (the principle of Eros), all these are associated with the goddess.

The goddess was considered virginal. In our modern understanding it is paradoxical to view the goddess as virginal when she is identified with passion and many lovers. But there is no paradox; in Latin *virgo* means unmarried, while *virgo intacta* refers to the lack of sexual experience. Today, the word "virgin" simply carries the latter meaning.

The virginal attribute of the goddess simply means she belongs to no man; rather she belongs to herself. She is not seen as a counterpart

---

[8] *The Homeric Hymns*, p. 71.

[9] Quoted in Christine Downing, *The Goddess: Mythological Images of the Feminine*, p. 204.

[10] Ibid., p. 205.

to other gods or as the feminine version of a god. Although she may be married, her husband is viewed as a consort. Her wifeliness does not alter her own attributes or lend her special status. The goddess of love exists in her own right, as "one-in-herself."[11] She is true to her own nature and instinct. One speaks of a virgin forest, which is free and unconstrained, pregnant with life in accordance with the laws of nature. It is untrammeled and untouched by man, or, we could say, the laws of man.[12] Likewise, the goddess of love behaved in accordance to her own divine laws of nature, free and unfettered by man-made laws.

The goddess of love was a moon goddess. In ancient times, in some of the locales where she was worshiped, the climate was hot and arid. The people presumed that as the torrid, blinding sun dried the land and destroyed the young green growth, it was the moon in her soft, shadowy illumination which offered life and abundance. The moon and her goddess were the fertilizing powers. Hence the goddess wore the crescent moon as a headdress, just as Isis is often depicted with crescent-shaped cowhorns and is therefore associated with the cow, the source of the milk of human kindness. In special religious festivals to the moon goddess, small cakes in the form of a crescent moon were used.

But the moon also had the power to bring lunacy. In the dark phase of the moon, the goddess was ominous in her boundless rage and ruthless destruction. Plutarch said of her, "The waxing moon is of good intent, but the waning moon brings sickness and death."[13] As the moon, she was cyclic, following a rhythm of constant change.

Another common thread which is intertwined in the myths of all the love goddesses is the theme of the son-lover, mentioned earlier. The goddess herself is eternal, yet the son-lover is slain or sacrificed to be resurrected again. Inanna's young love was the shepherd Dumuzi, who was sacrificed to the Nether World for six months every year, as was Ishtar's son-lover, Tammuz. In Egypt, there were Isis and Osiris, in Lydia, Cybele and Attis. The theme is repeated as each young man meets an untimely, cruel death, and eventually is brought to earth or life once again. It continues throughout the eras to the more familiar Greek mythology.

---

11 M. Esther Harding, *Woman's Mysteries: Ancient and Modern*, p. 124.

12 See John Layard, *The Virgin Archetype*.

13 Quoted in Harding, *Woman's Mysteries*, p. 114.

One Greek myth tells of Aphrodite and her beautiful Adonis (a name which means Lord and Master). Aphrodite finds Adonis at his birth out of a tree into which his mother had transformed herself. Aphrodite put the child in a coffer which she then entrusted to the goddess of the underworld, Persephone.

When later Aphrodite came to reclaim the coffer she found that Persephone had already opened it, beheld the great beauty of the child and refused to give him up. The dispute between the two goddesses was brought before Zeus, who resolved the conflict by deciding that Adonis should spend half the year on earth and half in the underworld.

During the part of the year he was with Aphrodite, she sought only to please him. Adonis had a passion for the chase, and even though Aphrodite feared some tragic fate would befall him, she could not discourage him.

One day, during a chase in the wild woods, Adonis was attacked and fatally gored by a boar. As Aphrodite rushed to him, she scratched her leg on a rose, which until that time had been white. The rose turned to red from her blood. (The red rose, a symbol of Aphrodite, is still very much thought of as a gift of love.) Aphrodite kissed Adonis as he died, and she felt herself to suffer the same piercing pain.

> Loss and death, unrequited love and abandonment, are all part of Aphrodite's realm. Indeed, only by these dark shadows does her golden brilliance become a complete creation, smiling its immortal smile as well as looking on death with immortal eyes. Permanence is of Hera's world, not Aphrodite's. What belongs to her is a deep acceptance that passionate love does not last forever; and an equally deep acceptance that man is made to love.[14]

This myth, like many others of the son-lover, may be interpreted simply as telling a metaphorical story about seasonal changes—the dying of vegetation in winter months, followed by the renewal of green growth in spring. Such an interpretation, however, overlooks the goddess' involvement, the depth of her emotion. All the myths of these goddesses emphasize the pain, the grief and the mourning they experienced over the death of the son-lover. We know the range of this goddess' emotions—joy and pleasure, yet also pain and grief—

---

[14] Arianna Stassinopoulos and Roloff Beny, *The Gods of Greece,* p. 83.

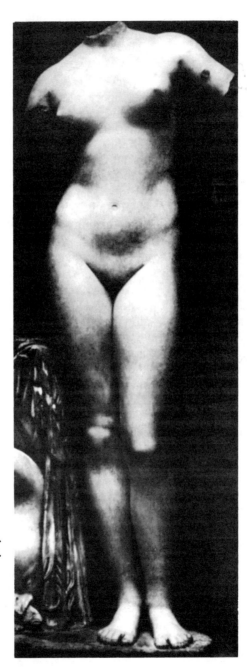

Aphrodite of Cyrene.
—Early Greek statue.

to a greater extent than those of all other goddesses. Emotions engendered by love's process are an integral part of her being.

*

⌈The woman who comes to know the goddess grows in the understanding of that divine aspect of her feminine nature that is part of the Self, the archetype of wholeness and the regulating center of the personality. Rather than trying to dominate her life, her ego works together with the Self. She is led, as it were, by her most profound needs, by ideals and attitudes that come from within. She is not contaminated by external circumstances or overly affected by criticism.⌉

For example, she finds her body beautiful and is consciously aware that it is, in part, a manifestation of the Self. "The Self, therefore, as the totality of the personality," notes Erich Neumann, "rightly bears the attributes of the exterior physical sex whose hormonal condition is closely connected with the psychological."[15] The body is not, as one woman expressed it, "simply a vehicle which takes my head from the house to the car," but prime matter by which she can come to know and to value her own deep emotions, intuitions and instinctive wisdom.

The woman conscious of the goddess cares for her body with proper nutrition and exercise and enjoys the ceremonies of bathing, cosmetics and dress. This is not just for the superficial purpose of personal appeal, which is related to ego gratification, but out of respect for the nature of the feminine. Her beauty derives from a vital connection to the Self.

Such a woman is virginal. This has nothing to do with a physical state, but with an inner attitude. She is not dependent on the reactions of others to define her own being. The virginal woman is not just a counterpart to the male, whether father, lover or husband. She stands as an equal in her own right. She is not governed by an abstract idea of what she "should" be like or "what people will think." Esther Harding writes:

> The woman who is virgin, one-in-herself, does what she does—not
> because of any desire to please, not to be liked, or to be approved,
> . . . not because of any desire to gain power over another, to catch
> his interest or love, but because what she does is true. . . . As virgin
> she is not influenced by the considerations that make the nonvirgin

---

[15] "Psychological Stages of Feminine Development," *Spring 1959*, p. 65.

woman, whether married or not, trim her sails and adapt herself to expediency. . . . She is what she is because that is what she is.[16]

If the motive for a woman's valuing of virginity in this sense is mere egocentricity, that would simply lead to a state of regression and a most undisciplined or uncivilized situation. "But when the motive is not a personal one but is concerned with a nonpersonal goal, namely with gaining a right relation to the 'goddess,' to the principle of Eros, the result is freed from egotism and selfishness."[17]

Philo of Alexandria, a first-century Jewish philosopher, described the true meaning of woman's virginal nature:

> For it is fitting God should converse with an undefiled, an untouched and pure nature, with her who in very truth is *the* Virgin, in fashion very different from ours. For the congress of men for the procreation of children makes virgins women. But when God begins to associate with the soul, He brings it to pass that she who was formerly woman becomes virgin again.[18]

The woman who knows the moon goddess is conscious of her own moon phases. She is aware of the cyclic rhythms in her body, and intuitively moves with the ebb and flow of changing energy or moods. The menstrual flow, echoing the moon's cycle, is confirmation of her fruitfulness, those creative abilities which are both physical and psychological. She acknowledges her own moon nature. There are times when she knows herself to be bright and illuminating, times which foster new growth. In the dark phase, she becomes aware of her black, foreboding, witchlike side, and is able to discharge this powerful energy in ways that are not destructive. She understands her need for extraverted times of shining forth as well as for times of seclusion and introspection. Both are comfortable positions when she is in harmony with the her own unique rhythms.

Sacrifice of the Son-Lover

The woman who is true to her inner goddess instinctively knows the need for the sacrifice of the son. The son-lover phenomenon can

---

16 *Woman's Mysteries,* pp. 125f. See also Marion Woodman, *The Pregnant Virgin: A Process of Psychological Transformation,* pp. 76, 126ff.

17 Harding, *Woman's Mysteries,* p. 126.

18 Ibid., p. 187.

be viewed in several ways. In external reality, it is common to see a mother who lives her life vicariously through her son. His achievements are her achievements; her goals and aspirations are not to establish a place in the world for herself but to have her son do this for her. Mother and son are then bound in a helpless symbiotic relationship, a state where neither can develop individually.

A similar situation occurs when a woman (who may not have biological sons) carries her insecurity into every relationship with a man; her maternal attitude "adopts" the son. She finds ways whereby the man becomes ever more dependent on her: through seemingly innocent and kindly gestures such as always seeking to help him, through indulgence or through an overly solicitous attitude. By creating a sense of helplessness in the male she elevates herself to a superior position.

In both situations, the son is sacrificed—but without redemption or transformation. The sacrifice is made not to life, but to the woman's ego desire for power. She lacks connection to the inner strength of the goddess, which demands a different sacrifice of the son, a sacrifice which would sever the unhealthy bonds and set him free.

In the myth of Inanna, when the goddess ascends from the Nether World where she has undergone a grueling transformation, she is commanded to provide an equal to take her place. Two *galla*, demons of the underworld, accompany Inanna to be sure that she does so. Inanna finds her lover Dumuzi in his shining garments sitting on a magnificent throne—there is no sign that he is mourning her absence. Inanna cries, "Take him away!" and the *galla* seize him. The myth continues, speaking of her weeping and mourning period: "Gone is my husband, my sweet husband. Gone is my love."[19]

Although it appears contradictory that the goddess instigated the sacrifice of her son-lover yet mourned his loss, as if she had second thoughts, the process is psychologically sound and stands to reason.[20] Mourning is a way of consciously integrating the fact that circumstances have changed; what was, is no longer, and it is not possible to have things as they once were. As a ritual, mourning assists necessary changes for development throughout life. If one has not

---

[19] Diane Wolkstein and S.N. Kramer, *Inanna: Queen of Heaven and Earth,* p. 86.

[20] See Sylvia Brinton Perera, *Descent to the Goddess: A Way of Initiation for Women,* pp. 81ff.

sacrificed the idealization of childhood, for instance, and lived a period of mourning to accept its loss, one remains a constant seeker of protection and security, unprepared for the risk and danger of the external world.

When there is a breakup of a relationship, if one attempts to replace the deep pain of mourning with fantasies of the partner's return, then life comes to a standstill. Even within a partnership that endures, old expectations must be sacrificed if each individual is to develop psychologically. This can result in much discontent, upheaval and sadness, again a mourning time. The death and mourning at least have a purpose, that of allowing regeneration in the relationship. Without the process of confronting old assumptions, regardless of how painful, the relationship is dead in any case.

The strength of the goddess lies in the capacity to give up that which is most precious, in order to ensure growth and regeneration; transformation can only take place when old attitudes and values give way to new ones. Hers is not a cold, calculating strength, denying all emotion; on the contrary, she feels the deepest emotions and does not restrict her mourning.

This is perhaps the most difficult aspect of the goddess to comprehend and certainly to integrate, for it goes against our cultural teachings. The active, dynamic aspect of feminine nature, that which promotes change and transformation, counterbalances the static, elemental aspect, the maternal, which, although it provides for growth, is essentially conservative and protective. Both are equally important in psychological development. Both must be consciously integrated if a woman is to to be open to healthy possibilities in specific circumstances. When to protect and nurture? When to let go of relationships or attitudes? To deal with such questions requires an intricate balance.

In the male's psychological development, a similar attitude toward the sacrifice of the son-lover is necessary. Since the boy infant's primary relationship is with the protective, nurturing mother, the boy first identifies with the feminine. This relationship is comfortable and undemanding; however, it creates a childish and dependent ego. The capacity to view oneself as "other than," where masculine ego consciousness is dominant, requires the sacrifice of sonship; the "son" here is that psychological (or physical) aspect which remains dependent on women for security, acceptance and nurture. The problem for the male is to free himself from fixation at the Oedipal stage or, in later life, from regressing to it.

An example of this complex transition is described in Robertson Davies' novel, *Fifth Business*. The narrator of the story tells of his conflicting feelings toward his mother:

> She did not know how much I loved her, and how miserable it made me to defy her, but what was I to do? Deep inside myself I knew that to yield, and promise what she wanted, would be the end of anything that was any good in me.[21]

Other examples of the man freeing himself from the mother are offered in mythology, although not so gently expressed as in the passage above. In one version of the myth of Cybele and Attis, the jealous, vengeful goddess induces delirium in Attis, the son-lover. In a frenzied state, Attis castrates himself and flings his dismembered testicles in the face of the mother goddess. This myth paints a very graphic picture of the necessary sacrifice of the son to make rebirth of the man possible.[22] Once free of the possessive mother, a man is then able to enter into a mature relationship with a woman.[23]

The man who has not separated from the mother views a woman as only an object which, on demand, immediately gratifies his sexual desires. This gratification is ephemeral; it passes quickly, and with such an attitude toward the feminine the spiritual dimension of the sexual act is never experienced. The heart is not touched; the soul is not nourished. Aphrodite embodies not just instinct, but also the soul's desire. In a mature alliance, the partners realize both the erotic and the spiritual potential of the relationship.

In Jungian terms, the anima, which means soul in Latin, is the personification of the contrasexual side of a man's unconscious—his own inner feminine nature, the *soulful* element in his psyche. She is the inner guide which leads the man through the labyrinth of the unconscious to the ultimate center of his being, the Self. The goddess is analogous to the "opposite other," the feminine element which together with the masculine comprises the totality of the Self.

According to Erich Neumann, the anima is "the vehicle par excellence of the transformative character" in a man. "It is the mover, the

---

[21] *Fifth Business,* p. 69.

[22] Harding, *Woman's Mysteries,* p. 193.

[23] This theme is developed in Eugene Monick, *Phallos: Sacred Image of the Masculine,* pp. 51ff.

instigator of change, whose fascination drives, lures, and encourages the male to all the adventures of the soul and spirit, of action and creation in the inner and the outward world."[24] Her image inspires an emotional response in both positive and negative measure. She may be experienced as *femme inspiratrice,* a loving creative muse, or as *femme fatale,* a snaring seductress. Her personifications range from the profane prostitute to Sophia, spiritual Wisdom.[25]

The stage of anima development in a man is concretely reflected in his external relationships with women. When he views the female as a sinister threat, someone to distrust, or as an inferior species which must be kept in its place, it is a sign that his inner feminine nature is still at a juvenile stage, ready to tease and taunt the male. Such a man steels himself against emotions lest they manifest in oversentimentality or inappropriate aggression. The inner feminine and relationships with women develop reciprocally when he is able consciously to value the feminine. Both the inner and outer woman may then be recognized as the embodiment of joy, passion, inspiration, creativity, spirituality and, in the highest order, Wisdom.

A mature anima manifests in a man's veneration for the strength and capacity of the love goddess. In the opening lines of Euripides' *Hippolytus*, Aphrodite says, "Those that respect my power I advance to honor, but bring to ruin all who vaunt themselves at me."[26] Aphrodite continues, speaking of Hippolytus: "He spurns love and will have nothing to do with sex. . . . It is his sinful neglect of *me* for which I shall punish Hippolytus this very day."[27]

*

For individuals unwilling to change narrow collective attitudes— especially those based on the laws of the patriarchy—psychological maturity is not possible. The neglect of the goddess results in a sterile, abrasive encounter with life; dullness and a lack of purpose creep in. A compulsive need for power replaces the joy of love. When feminine nature is valued, not seen as a toy to be played with but as an energy to be embraced, psychic life blossoms and becomes fruitful, bringing a new perspective.

---

[24] *The Great Mother: An Analysis of the Archetype,* p. 33.
[25] This is discussed below, in chapter 3.
[26] Paul Friedrich, *The Meaning of Aphrodite,* p. 94.
[27] Stassinopoulos and Beny, *The Gods of Greece,* p. 82.

The goddess of love, the archetypal image of a particular kind of psychic energy, is a most powerful goddess. Her realm is as extensive as the Heavens and the Earth, the mysterious world of the divine and our external reality. The laugh-loving, radiant goddess is a vital psychic principle in both men and women. She is the active principle of Eros which enables us to be related to our own emotions, and also to touch the emotional substance of another.

The goddess is the bringer of love and rapture. She combines the natural instinctive sexual drive and the highly cultivated art of love-making. "Aphrodite's essence is transformation through the power of beauty and love—the [psychic] power that is responsible for all metamorphoses."[28]

The Sacred Prostitute

As described in the first chapter, the sacred prostitute is a mortal woman who is devoted to the goddess. Her beauty, her graceful movements, her freedom from ambivalence, anxieties or self-consciousness toward her sexuality, all attributes of the goddess as well, derive from the reverence she holds for her feminine nature.

The sacred prostitute may be considered an archetypal image in that her energy is associated with specific emotions and patterns of behavior—but she is also human. The goddess of love and the sacred prostitute belong to one principle, the principle of Eros; yet the principle itself is both human and divine. This concept parallels Christian belief in the duality of the Father and Son, who are nevertheless One. Christ, the Son, is the aspect closer to humanity; through Him one comes to know the Father. "No one cometh unto the Father, but by me."[29]

Similarly, we can amplify the meaning of the goddess and realize the psychological implications of the image, but because it is archetypal it can never be fully integrated into consciousness. We cannot enter the realm of the gods or identify with their power; that leads to insanity, to the overwhelming of the human ego. Through the sacred prostitute we come to realize the attributes of the goddess of love. We may then consciously integrate into our human lives the significance of her characteristic qualities.

---

[28] Ibid., p. 83.
[29] John 14:6.

Mythology offers an example of a mortal woman who was associated with the divine—Ariadne, the daughter of King Minos of Crete. Many stories surround this perfect image of beauty, as she was often designated. In one well-known version of the myth, Ariadne falls in love at first sight with the handsome hero, Theseus, and declares that she will help his deliverance from the labyrinth if he promises to take her away from Crete and make her his wife. She cleverly provides Theseus with a ball of thread which marks his route out of the complex maze, and thus he is saved from being eaten by the monster Minotaur.

Theseus takes Ariadne with him away from Crete but then abandons her on a desolate island. Alone, she is broken hearted and suffers terrible sorrow. As she laments, the god Dionysus appears to raise her up to be the queen of his realm.

There are other associations with Ariadne, perhaps less commonly known, and although she was never designated as a sacred prostitute per se, strong parallels suggest that her relation to the goddess was of a similar character. Frequently she was referred to as "Ariadne Aphrodite." Moreover, she wears the crown of Aphrodite, which according to one version of the myth Theseus brought from the bottom of the sea, the birthplace of Aphrodite. On Attic vase paintings of Ariadne we find the Greek word meaning "the most holy," precisely the title which honored Aphrodite on Delos.[30]

Ariadne supposedly brought the carved statue of Aphrodite from Crete to Delos, established a temple to the goddess and was prominent in the goddess' worship there, especially in the famous dance of the Delian festivals.[31]

---

[30] Walter Otto, *Dionysus: Myth and Cult,* p. 183. Otto states, "The word "holy" can only lead Christian readers into error. The translation 'pure,' which is just as close, is unsatisfactory because our concept of purity can hardly be separated from its moral connotations. The words 'untouched' and 'untouchable' get us closest to the real meaning, but by this we must think of the untouchability and untouchableness of a nature which is removed from man and is foreign to his concept of good as well as of evil. This is a nature which is close to the divine, and it is for this reason that the concept of untouchableness is associated simultaneously with that which inspires worship."

[31] Ibid., pp. 181f.

Ariadne is also depicted as leader of the ecstatic dancing maenads, the women followers of Dionysus.[32] The dancing is not unlike the bacchanalian dance of the sacred prostitute. Plutarch explains that the dance was a madness filled with prophecy and a secret knowledge.[33] The dancing body enters into a ritual which connects the personal and the transpersonal; through erotic ecstasy the profundity of the spirit is realized.

Another place where Ariadne is the overseer of women's rituals is in the Villa of Mysteries of ancient Pompeii. The villa, located about a mile out of the town, is removed from the secular goings-on of daily life. It was a place specifically for the initiation of women. The main hall is decorated with a bold and exquisite frieze on all four walls, paintings unaltered since before the Christian era. Depicted on the frieze is the story of the initiation process, and there, as if presiding over the ceremony, is the regal, calm and thoughtful Ariadne, seated on the luxuriant marriage couch. To her right is the image of Dionysus, god of the vine. Human and divine are both present.

The first stage of initiation depicted in the frieze begins with the preliminaries of prayer, the ritual meal and purification. The second stage is entrance into the underworld, showing half-human, half-beast satyrs and Silenus, a fat old drunken man yet one endowed with immense knowledge of past and future. With the loosening of consciousness, the initiate entered the world of instincts and wisdom far from rational safety. The painting depicts fear in the initiate's face, and her position suggests that she wishes to escape; yet she drinks of the Dionysian wine held by Silenus.

In each successive stage the initiate is less clothed, as if she were divesting herself of old roles in order to receive a new image of herself. In the final stage a winnowing basket containing the ritual phallus is unveiled to her; she is now able to look upon the fertilizing power of the god, a primal regenerative force. This is not without danger, however, for if the powerful magnetism of masculine nature so mesmerizes her that she remains in the realm of the god, she loses the rightful connection to feminine consciousness and her femininity.

---

[32] Ibid., p. 177. Otto considered the maenads to be an archetypal image of womanliness, expressed in their magical beauty, motherliness, music, prophecy and association with death. For this reason, he writes, "It would be impossible to think of them as possessed with the same excessive erotic desire found in men."

[33] Ibid., p. 144.

Ariadne.
(The Villa of Mysteries, Pompeii)

A winged goddess with a long, flaying whip stands over the initiate, who submits in humility. Also in this scene is an older woman who wears the cap of knowledge, as one who has been initiated and in whose lap the kneeling initiate lays her head. She does not protect the novice, but is there in support of her.

The pain and humbling experience of the total ritual is connected back to the human woman; the initiate is not in an inflationary state of ego aggrandizement, but carries the mysteries within her innermost soul. The final scene shows the initiate beautifully dressed and adorned. She grooms herself in the mirror of Eros, which reflects her feminine nature of relatedness. She has entered into and experienced, and now embodies, the sacred marriage of Ariadne and Dionysus. She is the woman transformed, ready to move into the outer world in full awareness of her deep inner strength.

Ariadne, a mortal woman, felt the same emotions as the goddess in the loss of the hero-lover. After the mourning she then was united with the god in the sacred marriage. Her story tells of the mystery of initiation of a maiden into womanhood.

In a woman's psychology this myth is analogous to a process whereby a woman frees herself from identification with the role of the father's daughter. Initially she is his "princess." To overcome this perpetual maidenhood, the hero, like a knight in shining armor, comes to rescue her from the confines of the father world. The hero is spirited and adventuresome, therefore bringing creative thoughts and new attitudes. The woman is no longer bound by the collective conscious attitude of the "old king" father principle.

A maiden of any age regularly projects her creative abilities onto a man, seeing herself only as reflected in her lover's eyes and accomplishments. She falls in love with the hero, embodiment of her own unconscious potential, and the man fights her battles, carries out her wishes or takes her out of an undesirable situation.

Falling in love is always a result of projection; it is not a mature feeling of respect and appreciation for the other; rather one loves an aspect of oneself. When the partner does not live up to the demands of the projection (and no human possibly can), the projection cannot be sustained; the reality of the person is seen and one wonders, "What did I ever see in him (or her)?"

For the woman to become more than just a reflection of her lover, the projection must be consciously withdrawn—abandoned or sacrificed. She must come to realize that the qualities she sees in him are actually inside herself. At that point she can also begin to appreciate the mature strength of the masculine, the god within, without losing the connection with her feminine nature. In the joining of opposite principles, the mature woman experiences the fertilization of her own creative energy.⚹

Although we no longer observe the formal initiation rites of sacred prostitution or those enacted at the Villa of Mysteries, they nevertheless occur on the psychic level. In dreams, active imagination or fantasy, the archetypal pattern of initiation is activated when one is ready. Jung speaks of "big dreams," which at certain stages of psychological development function as did ancient religious rituals, to move one toward personal wholeness.

The following is a dream of an adult woman who, although very bright and competent, had not lived life fully. By choice she had remained single. She enjoyed many friends yet had never engaged in a sexual or love relationship, and was, as she stated in her initial analytic session, "afraid of men." The dream occurred on New Year's Eve, a time symbolic of new beginnings.

> I am in a room and the walls begin to change. It becomes another place. This would come in waves, over and over again. I learned to recognize the first signs of this experience because a picture, a table or a lamp would start to melt, and then the whole room would begin to undulate. The room would then transform into another place, and strange things would begin to occur. I would have to be of two minds to survive the experience. For instance, I would have to literally hold on to my body to keep it from being sucked into some swirling vortex of energy. At the same time I had to allow this to happen in order for the experience to continue.
>
> During one of the episodes (after the room changed), a long vine with leaves on it wrapped itself round and round my body. It wasn't hard to extricate myself from the vine and I threw it to the floor where it immediately became a snake. It attacked me between my legs. I jumped away just as it touched me but it sent a shock throughout my body.

This dream occurred at a time in the woman's life when rational understanding was in a state of flux and there were few familiar points of orientation. The "swirling vortex of energy" is analogous to the chaotic, undifferentiated unconscious, within which the dreamer is able to remain connected with herself through her body. The vine symbolizes the god Dionysus, whose phallic power manifests in the snake that penetrates the maidenhead. The snake is also associated with healing, wisdom and transformation. It was a powerful dream, akin to an initiation ritual. It had a powerful effect on this woman; her conscious attitudes and her image of herself were transformed.

Like Ariadne, the sacred prostitute is an archetypal image of one who has been initiated into the mysteries and achieved a profound connection with the goddess of love. Having integrated the goddess' potency, she can then mediate the demands of the unconscious to other females when the safety of conventional structures is called into question.

The sacred prostitute is therefore that human woman who, through formal ritual or psychological development, has consciously come to know the spiritual side of her eroticism and lives this out according to her individual circumstances. We find her in all walks of life. One feels a certain *presence* in her midst, a combination of joy and wisdom. She is "one-in-herself," free of the confines of convention; she lives her life as she chooses.

Such a woman may not be considered sexy or provocative in the usual sense of these words, for her sexuality is not superficial, not motivated by conscious design or unconscious demands. It is not a learned behavior, an acquired skill or a matter of ability, but rather a subtlety of her being springing from the depths of her soul. Her countenance holds a power, "a mysterious power that everyone feels but that no philosopher has explained."[34]

The sacred prostitute is also an aspect of the man's anima, the internal feminine image that would lead a man to value aspects of himself that involve erotic spirituality. She is a dancing, radiant, exciting image of the feminine, one which he must (as discussed in the next chapter) become consciously aware of *as an internal image,* if he is to have a loving relationship with an actual woman.

The Stranger

The stranger who came to the temple to worship the goddess of love in intercourse with the sacred prostitute was in ancient times viewed as an emissary of the gods, or even the god in disguise.

The archetype of the stranger functions in a similar manner in the psychological process. It is an image found often in myths, religion

---

[34] Federico Garcia Lorca, "Theory and Function of the Duendè," in Donald Allen and Warren Tallman, eds., *Poetics of the New American Poetry,* p. 91.

and fairy tales, as well as dreams, pointing to an aspect of the unconscious which breaks through into consciousness to instigate change. Whenever it appears there is indeed a feeling of strangeness, as something "other than" enters in and the numinosity of the divine is experienced.

In Teutonic mythology the god Wotan disguised as a beggar would knock on the door of a poor unsuspecting mortal. Depending on how he was received, the household would be richly blessed or would fall desolate under the curse of the wrathful god. In Jewish tradition, during the religious celebration of the Seder, an empty place is set and a chair is placed in readiness to receive the uninvited guest, the stranger who may come. These preparations are for the prophet Elijah, the emissary of God, who is to announce the coming of the Messiah.

In Christian tradition, the stranger appeared before Mary, announcing that the Holy Ghost would come upon her and that she would conceive the Son of God. It was also two strangers, men in shining garments waiting at the empty tomb, who revealed to the women who came that the crucified Jesus had risen from the dead.

A common motif in fairy tales is one in which the stranger comes to knock on the door of a poor man's house to request that his beautiful daughter go with him. In return the daughter will realize great wealth and the father's household will know no need. In the tale, "East of the Sun and West of the Moon," it is a beast-stranger, an enormous white bear, who comes to the door with such a request, and because of terrible poverty the father reluctantly agrees.

Saddened to leave her father's house, the daughter travels to a distant land on the back of the beast and remains with him there, where every comfort is provided. After a time she wishes to return to her home, and while she is visiting there her mother plants destructive thoughts in her mind. Such notions bring about separation from the stranger-beast, the one she has grown to love. After successfully undergoing many trials and undertaking long journeys she is reunited with the stranger-beast, who at the end of the tale is transformed into a prince.

The stranger is typically one who is uninvited, unexpected and of foreign nature. He comes from an other-worldly place and instigates change. A numinous aura surrounds him. This is the essence of the stranger in the context of the initiation rituals enacted by the sacred prostitute: he facilitates her transition from the innocence of maidenhood to the realization of her full feminine nature. Psychologically, in a woman, it is a stage where the masculine principle breaks through:

> The woman is seized by an unknown, overwhelming power which she experiences as a formless "numinosum."[35]

> Through her total seizure by the masculine [principle] the woman overcomes the stage of self-conservation and arrives at a new phase of her experience. The orgiastic total seizure has a spiritual character, although it takes place in the body too. This spiritual character, however, has nothing to do with abstract logic of the masculine, patriarchal spirit, but belongs to a specifically feminine form of spiritual experience which in mythology is frequently connected with the moon symbol.[36]

In a woman's psychology, the male stranger is an aspect of what Jung called the animus, the contrasexual side of a woman's psyche—an inner man, so to speak.[37] At his best he functions as a bridge between the woman's ego and her own creative resources.[38] At worst, he manifests as opinions and assumptions that play havoc with her relationships.[39]

The word animus in Latin means spirit. The positive animus inspirits the woman, leading her out into the world of objects, creativity and ideas. It is that psychic function that enables a sense of direction, focus, discernment and ordered continuity in all endeavors.

The animus appears in many forms other than the stranger, such as the wise old man, a youthful Adonis, or even a baby boy, and each manifestation has a particular psychological meaning. In his negative form he may appear, for instance, as a rapist or as a robber

---

[35] Erich Neumann, "The Psychological Stages of Feminine Development," p. 70.

[36] Ibid., p. 72.

[37] See "The Syzygy: Anima and Animus," *Aion*, CW 9ii, pars. 20ff, where Jung writes: "[Woman's feminine consciousness] is compensated by a masculine element and therefore her unconscious has . . . a masculine imprint. . . . The animus corresponds to the paternal Logos just as the anima corresponds to the maternal Eros." (par. 29)

[38] See Irene Claremont de Castillejo, *Knowing Woman*, pp. 73ff.

[39] Jung, "Commentary on 'The Secret of the Golden Flower,'" *Alchemical Studies*, CW 13, par. 60: "On a low level the animus is an inferior Logos, a caricature of the differentiated masculine mind, just as on a low level the anima is a caricature of the feminine Eros." See also "The Syzygy: Anima and Animus," *Aion*, CW 9ii, par. 29.

who takes the woman's most prized possessions, symbolic of her feminine nature.

Coming to know and differentiate the various guises of the animus involves undergoing something akin to the initiation rite referred to above, where the woman is seized and penetrated by the masculine spirit. It is not only a psychological process but involves the body as well.

> The connection of the spiritual seizure with a physical paroxysm is expressed in the modern woman in the fact that she can experience an orgasm with spiritual excitement, for example, with music, and that her "understanding" of spiritual contents also can be combined with bodily sensations. This means that she understands, symbolically speaking, not with the head but with the whole body, and that in her spiritual and corporal processes are bound together in a way quite foreign to the average man.[40]

A woman in her early thirties had the following dream. She had been indiscriminately sexually active—which she referred to as "ball-bursting"—for several years since her divorce. Several months prior to the dream she began to feel a deep emptiness, and described her chest as being bound by a "chain of tears." She spent much time in self-reflection, attempting to connect to the woman crying inside herself. Her dream came during this time.

> I am cleaning my house, and then bathing and dressing myself because a most distinguished guest is coming although I do not know who it will be. I feel the extreme importance and am nervous. The ambassador from Japan arrives. We greet each other cordially, although I am still nervous. He performs the tea ceremony for me. We enter the bedroom (not my own in reality) and make love. With no words spoken, he leaves and I remain in a state of ecstasy.

This dream reflects the concerted effort made by the woman to understand what was going on in herself. Her psychic housecleaning and the ritual purification of her body prepare her to receive the important guest from the "other world," symbolic of the stranger animus. This emissary of the divine performs a ritual through which the dignity of relationships is honored. Their union is ecstatic—transpersonal and transformative.

---

[40] Neumann, "Stages of Feminine Development," p. 72.

Women who are sexually promiscuous, lacking an emotional tie or even harboring a deep resentment toward their partner, are unrelated to their essential feminine nature. That is precisely the situation which feeds the negative animus. The animus is as negative in the inner life of such a woman as are her views of men in her outer life. He turns a cruel face toward her, undercutting her every move. The more adamantly she believes that men are her enemies, the less she is able to realize that the enemy is within herself. There is no ritual preparation, such as the above dreamer experienced, no welcome reception of the mysterious Other.

Likewise, women who experience sexual anxieties have never fully experienced the breakthrough, the penetration, of the masculine. Such women remain, as it were, like the girl in the fairy tale, living in the emotional impoverishment of the father's house. Their fears of the phallic beast prevent them from experiencing love and its transforming effects, not only on themselves but on their partners. The inner animus remains in an undeveloped state, forever a frog, never recognized as the prince it could become.

The positive stranger animus enables a woman to focus on and to discern the attributes and beauty of her feminine nature. He guides her into the conscious realization of her femininity. She then has the ability to make choices that do not compromise it. Just as the sacred prostitute went out into the world when the ritual was completed, prepared to enter marriage as a person fully aware of her capacity, so the modern woman who has integrated her animus is prepared for life.

Whatever she undertakes, she does so with confidence, without regression, submissiveness or a feeling of inferiority to a patriarchal system (which would mean returning to the father's house). She neither has to compete with men nor adopt masculine qualities, that is, identify with the animus. The woman who has come to know the presence of the masculine power within is her own authority and stands constant to her feminine nature. She may not be able to change the patriarchal system which surrounds her, but, more importantly, she doesn't allow the system to change her.

The Marriage Ritual

In the ancient world, the climax of the prolonged New Year's festival, as mentioned in chapter 1, was the celebrated ritual of the sacred marriage. It was an exalted religious event reflecting devotion to the goddess of love.

Amid the feasting, dancing and rejoicing, a distinguished and favored sacred prostitute and the reigning monarch were joined in the symbolic marriage. The sacred prostitute was the embodiment of the goddess of love as the king was the personification of the god. In this joyous union, fecundity of land and womb, and the well-being of all people, were assured.

This religious ritual, like many others, was based on a psychological need. An essential spiritual dimension of life was projected outward and made concrete in the enactment of the sacred union. Two elements, male and female, were joined together in the presence of a third, the divine. The psychological need symbolized by the sacred marriage is the psyche's movement toward wholeness. The closest modern equivalent is the sacrament of Holy Matrimony.[41]

Psychologically, the sacred marriage symbolizes the union of opposites. It is the coming together, in equal status, of the masculine and feminine principles, the conjoining of consciousness and unconsciousness, of spirit and matter. It is a mystical process by which disconnected elements are joined together to form a whole. In the consummation of the *hieros gamos,* sexuality and spirituality are integral aspects, each drawing vitality from the other. This psychic process, writes Jung, brings about "the 'earthing' of the spirit and the spiritualizing of the earth, the union of opposites and reconciliation of the divided."[42]

The sacred marriage is an archetypal motif, and for this reason we find many examples of it in literature, legends and world religions. Common to many fairy tales is the royal wedding in which a prince and princess, each from a different country, are brought together by fortuitous circumstances and then united in marriage. The stories repeatedly involve a long search or heroic deeds, full of perils and fraught with hardship and despair.

One example is Grimm's tale, "The Three Feathers," which tells of an old, sick king who devises some competitive tasks to determine

---

[41] The difference between our cultural marriage and the sacred marriage is that the former is sociological, overlaid with legal implications, while the latter is a mystical union, essentially symbolic.

[42] "The Personification of the Opposites," *Mysterium Coniunctionis,* CW 14, par. 207.

which of his three sons will reign in his place after his death. The direction each son is to go to complete the tasks is settled by the toss of three feathers. One feather flies east and another west, and these are the routes two of the brothers take. One feather falls straight to the ground and the third prince, called Simpleton because he does not speak much, finds a little trapdoor through which he goes down into the earth. There he meets a fat toad who gives him beautiful prizes to win the competition. His brothers are stunned when he brings these precious objects to the surface.

The last task set by the old king is to find the most beautiful wife. Again the simple brother descends into the earth to solicit help from the fat toad, and she implores him to take his pick from the many little toads around. He chooses one at random, and on the way to the surface it is transformed into the most beautiful woman. The prince claims his bride and his father's kingdom.

Descending into the realm of the unconscious, down into the unknown, away from tried and true routes, is the first step in redeeming the potential treasures of one's personality. The old king in this story represents the dominant attitude of consciousness, which is worn out and needs to be renewed. There is no feminine element at the beginning of the tale, no queen or princess. This signifies the extent to which the feminine is excluded from conscious consideration. Just as the simpleton, symbolizing a naive, receptive attitude toward the unconscious, unquestioningly accepts a toad as his bride, so a man, in accepting his anima as he finds her, enables her transformation.

There are similar fairy tales, more obviously relevant to a woman's psychology, in which a princess must kiss a toad or proclaim her love for an ugly animal-man (as in "Beauty and the Beast"), at which point he turns into a handsome prince. In contacting the contrasexual side of oneself the usual rules of consciousness do not apply. As one accepts and embraces the Other, transformation takes place, not only on an unconscious level but in the conscious realm as well. The masculine and feminine principles, Logos and Eros, are united, coequals in consciousness.

In other instances, the image of the sacred marriage is more abstract, but the psychological meaning remains the same. Wagner's final masterpiece, *Parsifal,* based on a very old Breton legend, depicts the separation of the Holy Grail and the Holy Spear.[43] The spear,

---

[43] *The Simon and Schuster Book of the Opera,*   p. 284.

taken from the place of the grail, falls into the hands of an evil magician and becomes the instrument which wounds the good Amfortas, King of the Grail Castle. Only the spear itself can heal the unbearable, painful wound of the ailing king and restore the Grail Castle, which has fallen into distress and misery.

After a long and arduous search, Parsifal, described as the pure fool (for he knows neither himself nor from where he comes), returns the spear to the castle and the king is healed. The Holy Grail and the Holy Spear are contained within the castle. Parsifal is then ordained as King of the Grail. He lifts the Grail, the source of new life and strength, which radiates a shining light through which a white dove descends and blesses the knights of the kingdom.

The Grail, as container, is symbolic of the feminine; the spear is symbolic of the masculine. Without the presence of the feminine, the masculine principle is wounded and the quality of life deteriorates. The feminine cannot be recognized (unveiled, as depicted in the opera). Consequently, the source of life's renewal is unavailable. Only through the efforts of a "pure fool," one not bound by collective ego rationalizations, the one who can serve a power greater than the ego, can the two principles be reunited and healing occur.

The Parsifalian search is again the story of the individuation process in which the symbols of the masculine and feminine principles are eventually conjoined, and wherein the divine, symbolized by the dove, enters. The white dove is symbolic not only of the Holy Ghost but also of the goddess of love, Aphrodite.

In Western religious tradition, there are numerous symbols of the union of opposites. The Holy Eucharist is one. A piece of the host, representing the body, is mingled with the wine, representing the spirit, thus producing the union or *coniunctio* of soul and body. A similar idea exists in classical Chinese philosophy, where the Tao signifies complete harmony between heaven and earth, spirit and matter, masculine and feminine. This concept is symbolized visually in the well-known design of the yin-yang: contained within the circle of wholeness is a black side with one white spot and a white side with a black spot. Each part contains an element of the other; the two together form the whole.

In order for a union to take place, two distinct opposites must exist. The masculine and feminine principles must first be differentiated. Differentiation is the psyche's work in the first half of life.[44] Initially, feminine and masculine are contained in the unconscious, the *prima materia;* no separateness is experienced. Through stages of development, physical as well as psychological differences become more clearly defined.[45]

Differentiation is not a limiting factor; on the contrary, it is necessary for full psychological development. In the second half of life, the psychic process is predisposed toward reuniting the opposites, only now on a conscious level where the feminine principle of Eros and the masculine principle of Logos function congruently. Alchemists from the time of the Dark Ages describe this process in the poetic image of Sol and Luna, as gold and silver, being melted into a unity purified of all opposition, and therefore incorruptible. But this sacred marriage can only occur after there has been a differentiation of the masculine and the feminine principles. As Ann Ulanov writes:

> Without wrestling with this task of differentiation, we fall into formlessness and a cheap imitation of current persona roles. We miss our chance to become unique persons. Furthermore, we miss the spiritual significance of physical sexuality. If we deny sexual differences we deny the fact of otherness that is so strikingly conveyed to all of us through sexual experience.[46]

A primitive legend conveys the necessity of differentiating and then reuniting opposites:

> The sky was the father and the earth was the mother; the two were forever lying in union, the sky weighing down upon the earth. Whatever offspring resulted therefrom were smothered by the weight of the father. But one day, one of the sons managed to work his way out, so he pierced the sky with his spear, raising it high above the earth. The pair were separated, but they were no longer fruitful. Another son, realizing the cause of the parents' sterility, came and married them according to the rite of the tribe.[47]

---

[44] See "The Stages of Life," *The Structure and Dynamics of the Psyche,* CW 8, pars. 749-795, where Jung writes about developmental stages in the first and second halves of life. The first half of life—not restricted to chronological years—is essentially involved with issues of separation from the parental figures, moving out into the world and establishing one's own ego identity. The second half of life involves dealing with the unconscious..

[45] See Neumann, "Stages of Feminine Development," p. 65.

[46] *The Feminine in Jungian Psychology and in Christian Theology,* p. 147.

[47] B.F. Goldberg, *The Sacred Fire: The Story of Sex in Religion,* p. 46.

Also related to the concept of the sacred marriage are love poems of all ages. Such poems express not only the longing two individuals feel for each other, but, in metaphysical terms, the longing of one's fractured being to be united with the inexplicable dimensions of the Self. In "The Canonization," one of his most famous poems, John Donne writes:

> Call us what you will, we are made such by love;
> Call her one, me another fly,
> We're tapers too and at our own cost die;
> And we in us find th' eagle and the dove.
> The phoenix riddle hath more wit
> By us: we two, being one, are it.
> So to one neutral thing both sexes fit;
> We die and rise the same and prove
> Mysterious by this love.[48]

Love, as an aspect of the divine, is the causative agent instigating a realization of the Self in the union of opposites. "You can therefore say," writes Marie-Louise von Franz, "that in every deep love experience the experience of the Self is involved, for the passion and the overwhelming factor in it come from the Self."[49]

It appears, then, that the archetype of the sacred marriage is manifested on three levels: interpersonally, intrapersonally and transpersonally. The levels are distinct threads interweaving to form a richly designed fabric of life. Each has an effect on the other. What transpires on the conscious level also transpires in the personal unconscious and the deep collective unconscious. Each level of the psyche participates in the sacred marriage.

When there exists a deep, abiding love between two people, the spirit of the divine is present. One is aware of laugh-loving, smiling and radiant sensations as the goddess enhances feelings of well-being. One may also be connected to the sufferings and pain of unrequited love, which belong to the goddess too. In either case, a bond exists on the level of the Self. It is a love that doesn't say, "You will love me because I love you," or, "I'll become what you expect me to be so that you will love me." Such expectations and requirements are characteristic of a selfish, Self-less love; the true elements of the Self

---

[48] John Ball, ed., *From Beowulf to Modern British Writers*, p. 289.

[49] *Alchemy: Introduction to the Symbolism and the Psychology*, p. 202.

remain hidden to the individual and to the other. Therefore the divine is not present.

The sacred marriage on an interpersonal level exists when two people are open to dreams or despair in a shared experience, in which vulnerability is considered precious, and wherein belief in the other is acknowledged and communicated in any number of ways. Projections of the anima or animus are withdrawn; the other is more clearly seen and cherished for what he or she actually is. There is a sense of freedom to explore the profundity of one's true being in connection with a loving companion, thus allowing development and creativity. In the literal act of making love, the experience of "melting together," as the alchemists said, if only for a brief moment, is analogous to the consummation of the sacred marriage. The two are joined together in the presence of the divine third.

On the intrapsychic level, the union of opposites is very much a similar experience, only it takes place in inner reality as opposed to the outside world. When unconscious projections of the anima and animus are withdrawn and their qualities are integrated into consciousness, they are met with a mixture of fascination and fear, not unlike the feeling of meeting a potential lover for the first time. There is a feeling of ravishment, of breaking through, as described earlier. A sense of upheaval is experienced. One then begins to befriend the soul, the spirit. Rational and irrational functions become companions respecting and learning from one another. Seeds of creativity from the unconscious ripen to maturity in consciousness.

When the opposites are reconciled, creative impulses develop into actions: they are not simply mused about in a far-off dreamy manner. A responsibility toward one's development is grasped with new-found strength to carry it through. No longer can one sincerely blame external circumstances for one's failures. Instead a determination develops to *make* things happen, to feel new feelings, to re-image oneself.

When the sacred marriage takes place intrapersonally there are frequently dreams of a traditional marriage, with an unknown figure as the bride or bridegroom. An attractive older woman, embarking on a new career after the death of her husband, had the following dream:

> I am attending a great celebration. There are tables of food prepared. There is music somewhere in the background. I realize I am the honored guest and this preparation is for my wedding. Now I am dressed in a bridal gown. I do not know who I am to marry but the groom appears. (I do not know him in reality.) He is handsome,

smiling and strong. For a moment I fear he is too young for me. Then I feel everything is appropriate and proceed toward the altar on his arm.

Collective conscious attitudes—being too old, being a woman, having financial security with no need to earn a living—made the dreamer doubtful about pursuing a career. The dream allayed those fears, for in it she found an inner source of strength which she could now draw on.

Dreams may also depict the sacred marriage with images of sexual intercourse. The following is a dream of a man in his mid-fifties whose traditional marriage of twenty-two years was monotonous. Between him and his wife there was no genuine companionship, humor or even warm feelings. He often felt estranged in his own home; he did not look forward to returning there after a stressful work day. Marital sex offered no opportunity for substantial expressions of love, and there had been no other sexual partners in his life. He was thirsty for the elixir of life.

The psychological situation was one where he was cut off from feminine nature—there was no principle of Eros operating in his external world, and his inner world was heavy-handedly repressed by the convincing rationality of Logos. Here is his dream:

My wife and I were in a building on the corner of a small village. We were excited in preparing to make love with each other. Our actions were tied in with the impending birth of an heir to the governor. When the time came for the birth to occur, fire trucks were sounding off and the whole community was in a great state of excitement; so were we!

The dream speaks of excited preparations for the union of opposites, with the man's contrasexual feminine side personified by his wife. The new life is announced by the fire truck's sirens, related to the heat of passion, the blaze of desire. The passion, the excitement, the coming together of masculine and feminine, all are symbolic of the birth of the Divine Child. The heir-apparent to the governor, the hitherto ruling or dominant attitude of consciousness, would manifest as a new conscious attitude in which masculine Logos and feminine Eros would work together.

When the sacred marriage occurs on the intrapsychic level, long-standing attachments to collective beliefs and assumptions are loosened. One becomes open to new approaches to old problems, if indeed problems are continued to be seen as such. A sense of humor, an important ingredient of psychic health, can be developed. One is more able to empathize with other people, respecting differences. The masculine and feminine principles are recognized as equal partners in consciousness.

The psychological experience of the sacred marriage proceeds from external reality to inner reality and then to the Beyond. The Chinese book of wisdom, the I Ching, speaks of this phenomenon in hexagram 50, called "Ting/The Caldron":

> All that is visible must grow beyond itself, extend into the realm of the invisible. Thereby it receives its true consecration and clarity and takes firm root in the cosmic order.
>
> Here we see civilization as it reaches its culmination in religion. The *ting* serves in offering sacrifice to God. The highest earthly values must be sacrificed to the divine. But the truly divine does not manifest itself apart from man.[50]

On the transpersonal level, the sacred marriage extends beyond the boundaries of human understanding. One is united with the divine, the source and the power of love. Through the mystical union a portion of divine love is received and contained within oneself. In the act of sacrifice to a greater authority, earthly values, such as ego desires or identification with power, are transformed into a capacity to love on a plane which surpasses human reasoning.

Instinctual nature, embedded in the body, carries this wisdom; the head cannot comprehend what the heart knows. Instinctual nature is not only the vehicle for biological processes but it also conveys the emotional feeling-tones of life in a way that could well be described as the language of the soul.

Esther Harding provides the following description of the sacred marriage as it relates to a woman; it would also apply to the man who has integrated the anima:

> The ritual of the *hieros gamos* is religious. Through the acceptance of the power of instinct within her, while at the same time renouncing all claim to possessiveness in regard to it, a woman gains a new relation to herself. The power of instinct within her is recognized as belonging not to herself but to the nonhuman realm, to the goddess, whom she must serve, for whom her body must be a worthy vessel.

---

[50] Richard Wilhelm, tr., *The I Ching or Book of Changes*, p. 194.

From this experience is born the power to love another. Before she has undergone such an initiation, her love is no more than desire. . . . But when she has passed through an inner experience analogous to the ancient prostitution in the temple, the elements of desirousness and possessiveness have been given up, transmuted through the appreciation that her sexuality, her instinct, are expressions of a divine life force whose experience is of inestimable value, quite apart from their fulfillment on the human plane.[51]

Transpersonally, the sacred marriage involves the mystery of transformation from the physical to the spiritual and vice versa. Each person is connected to the universe as if one were a single cell in the organism of the planetary field of consciousness.[52] From the union of the human and the divine, the Divine Child is born. The Divine Child is new life—life with new understanding, life which carries an illuminating vision into the world.

*

The sacred prostitute and the rituals she willingly enacted represent a way of remaining connected through unconscious archetypal patterns to the instinctive energies of the goddess of love. Although now we seldom participate in rituals which allow us to be transformed by the divine, these significant happenings may still be realized psychologically—but only when the emotions which charge the images of the sacred prostitute, the goddess, the stranger and the sacred marriage are honored by conscious understanding.

---

[51] *Woman's Mysteries,* pp. 151ff.
[52] I am indebted to Jose Arguelles for these thoughts in his lecture, "The Principle of Organic Resonance," Union Graduate School, May 1986.

Auguste Rodin, *The Eternal Idol,* 1889.
(Musée Rodin, Paris)

3

The Sacred Prostitute
in Masculine Psychology

> All saints revile her, and all sober men
> Ruled by the God Apollo's golden mean—
> In scorn of which I sailed to find her
> In distant regions likeliest to hold her
> Whom I desired above all things to know,
> Sister of the mirage and echo.
> —Robert Graves, *The White Goddess.*

Anima: Man's Image of Woman

She has many faces, many guises. She has lived in the mind's eye of
man throughout the ages. The anima, man's inner image of woman,
manifests in each male according to his individual psychology.

> Every man carries within him the eternal image of woman, not the
> image of this or that particular woman, but a definite feminine im-
> age. This image is fundamentally unconscious, an hereditary factor
> of primordial origin engraved in the living organic system of the
> man, an imprint or "archetype" of all the ancestral experiences of the
> female.[1]

Like a witch, she can cast spells of moodiness, irritability or depression. Like the Greek Sirens or the German Lorelei, the anima can
lure a man to destruction.[2] On the positive side, she brings joy, excitement and a sense of well-being. Like the woman who tamed
Enkidu in the Gilgamesh Epic,[3] she may be seen as a reflection of a
man's inner woman capable of leading him out of "the wild life."

---

[1] Jung, "Marriage as a Psychological Relationship," *The Development of
Personality,* CW 17, par. 338.

[2] See Jung, *Man and His Symbols,* p. 178.

[3] See above, pp. 33-34.

Down through the ages men have attempted to unravel the mystery of their eternal image of woman. Her sexuality and spirituality inspire a unique fascination. Her exotic image has been captured on the canvas of Goya as the elegant, reclining nude, *The Naked Maja,* or as the *Sleeping Venus* by Giorgione whose pose expresses pure innocence without a trace of immodesty.

A similar enchantment with the feminine image is observed in the recently revealed series of the mysterious Helga by Andrew Wyeth. Rembrandt used his mistress as his model for the portrait he called *Juno,* and in his inspiration elevated her to the realm of the goddess. Titian's image was the bare-breasted, golden-haired woman full of rapture whom he named *Mary Magdalene.* Man's inner reflection of the feminine glows in the countless paintings and statues of Aphrodite and the equally numerous portrayals of the Virgin Mary.

Today, man's idea of woman continues to be displayed, though not often with the grandeur and reverence characteristic of classical art. Pornographic films and centerfolds in slick magazines reveal the inner woman of some modern men. Another of her images, coming from the far side of reality, is often mirrored in the poetry of contemporary song, as in "Suzanne" by Leonard Cohen:

> Suzanne takes you down by her place by the river.
> You can hear the boats go by.
> You can spend the night beside her.
> And you know that she's half-crazy,
> And that's why you want to be there,
> And she feeds you tea and oranges
> That come all the way from China.
> And just when you mean to tell her
> That you have no love to give her,
> She gets you on her wave length and lets the river answer
> That you've always been her lover.[4]

The male's internal image of the feminine ranges from the sensuous and exotic to the divine. Since the anima is a personification of the male's unconscious, it is her image that men regularly project onto the women in their lives.

The feminine in man not only excites him but acts as soul guide on his inner journey. She is Dante's Beatrice, for whose sake he embarks on a heroic adventure in the lower and upper worlds; in so

---

[4] "Suzanne" by Leonard Cohen, copyright 1966, Project Seven Music.

Goya, *The Naked Maja* (detail), c. 1800.

doing, he exalts his lady's image to the mystical image of the Mother of God. Or the soul guide can be more earthy, like the prostitute Hermine encountered by Harry Haller, the protagonist of Herman Hesse's *Steppenwolf*. Haller is a professed pacifist, but inwardly a devouring wolf. He lives secluded in a tiny room and is brought back into the tempo of life by Hermine. She teaches him to dance and to feel the harmonic rhythm of life's forces as she leads him from isolation to the throbbing world of emotions and appetites. Through her his inner wolf is made conscious. Hermine instills wisdom in Harry as she acquaints him with the neglected areas of his life.

Although great strides have been made in recent years to grant women equal status in the world, the patriarchal system continues to prevail and to impose masculine viewpoints and values on the image of woman. These values reflect the relationship the collective masculine world has both to external woman and to the internal anima. From this point of view, it appears the feminine has three faces—she is mother, whore or virgin—and often a combination of all three. The face the individual man sees is a reflection of his anima.

"When projected," writes Jung, "the anima always has a feminine form with definite characteristics. This empirical finding does not mean that the archetype is constituted like that *in itself.*"[5] Elsewhere he points out that "most of what men say about feminine eroticism, and particularly about the emotional life of women, is derived from their own anima projections and distorted accordingly."[6]

The woman may be viewed as "property," someone who exists to serve the man's sexual need. In that case she is his whore, his profane prostitute. In most instances such an attitude would be consciously denied; however, it regularly erupts in locker-room expressions, in the sexual harassment found in work situations, and in the privacy of the marriage bed. The repressed notion of woman-as-whore is frequently the manifest or hidden element in marital problems. The man who expects sexual gratification on demand from his wife, as his right and her duty, consciously or unconsciously envisions woman as his whore.

Quite the opposite is the situation where woman is elevated to the heavenly heights of The Virgin Mother; she is all things pure and

---

[5] "Concerning the Archetypes and the Anima Concept," *The Archetypes and the Collective Unconscious,* CW 9i, par. 142 (his emphasis).

[6] "Marriage As a Psychological Relationship," *The Development of Personality,* CW 17, par. 338.

holy, and consequently is untouchable. "Goddesses and demigoddesses," writes Jung, "took the place of the personal, human woman who should carry the projection of the anima."[7] In such cases, relationship with an actual woman is not possible. The projection shatters when the man discovers she is human after all. He then finds fault with his partner, leaves the relationship or becomes impotent. He may remain disheartened, disenchanted to the extent that he finds all women disreputable.

A classic example of this took place on a grand scale in the Middle Ages, when at the same time as magnificent cathedrals were being built to glorify the Virgin Mary, human women who stood solidly on the ground were being persecuted as witches.[8]

The third face of man's inner feminine composite is that of the mother-wife. "For the son," writes Jung, "the anima is hidden in the dominating power of the mother, and sometimes she leaves him with a sentimental attachment that lasts throughout life and seriously impairs the fate of the adult."[9]

Typically today, a man in the first half of life leaves the parental home and takes a wife to establish a home of his own. This is undeniably an important first step, for it is an active effort to free oneself from the anima fascination initially carried by the mother; however, sometimes the wife becomes simply a substitute mother.

As mentioned earlier, the image of woman as maternal is the elemental or static aspect of the feminine, associated with conservative and unchanging attitudes.[10] The security furnished by the stable situation presents a danger, for the man then lacks the experience and emotional challenges that foster anima development. Jung writes,

> The overwhelming majority of men on the present cultural level never advance beyond the maternal significance of woman, and this is the reason why the anima seldom develops beyond the infantile, primitive level of the prostitute. Consequently prostitution is one of the main by-products of civilized marriage.[11]

---

[7] "Mind and Earth," *Civilization in Transition,* CW 10, par. 76.

[8] See Jung, "The Type Problem in Poetry," *Psychological Types,* CW 6, par. 339.

[9] "Archetypes of the Collective Unconscious," *The Archetypes and the Collective Unconscious,* CW 9i, par. 61.

[10] See above, pp. 56ff.

[11] "Mind and Earth," *Civilization in Transition,* CW 10, par. 79.

It is not uncommon to hear a man speak of the change in the personal relationship he has with his wife once there are children. The man's image of the feminine, which previously had excited him in love-making, now regresses back to the static maternal model. He feels stuck, often without vitality or a sense of creativity.

Escalating divorce rates in the Western world reflect the route some men take to escape the domination of the wife-mother. Present-day societal norms offer no alternatives except divorce and secret affairs to alleviate the frustration and stress men feel when the passionate, dynamic aspect of the feminine is mired down in static maternal security.

The Anima in Dreams

The feminine within is literally the stuff dreams are made of. Most often the anima in dreams takes the form of an actual woman whose personal characteristics are significant to the dreamer. She may be someone with whom he is associated in outer life or someone totally unknown. From a still deeper realm of the unconscious come archetypal images of feminine nature, symbolic forms overlaid with emotion.

In the following dream, the goddess of love herself comes in symbolic form, as a dove. Paul was a forty-year-old Swiss man who had been twice divorced and was increasingly unhappy with a third partner. The dream illustrates on an archetypal level the denial of both the actual women and Paul's own inner feminine, symptomatic of his unconscious attitude toward the goddess and her gift of love.

> I was walking with E. I feel something in my hand I found in the street. I get the feeling that it comes to life. I call to E. who is now D. It turns into a pigeon. It blows itself up and walks around looking for some food. I have some crumbs in my pocket and give them to it in my hand. Later it changes into a white dove. I tell a young man, "You see it's like you, as near to death as to life."
>
> Later the dove is dying again. I'm in a room and the young man brings it in. "Look at your pigeon-dove." It's dead again and he throws it on the table. It's alive again and jumps to the floor. I think it's looking for a place to die calmly. The young man does not seem to have any feelings for that. I don't quite remember the next scene but there seems to be a link between the white dove and D., who is lying somewhere, dead.

In his associations, Paul identified E. as a playmate whom he had first met when he was five. Their friendship lasted throughout adolescence. She was his first girlfriend, and he recalled her with much fondness. With her he first became aware of love—Aphrodite, who is traditionally symbolized by a white dove. In the dream it is first a pigeon, of the same family as the dove yet not so evolved or refined. Paul's association with pigeons was that they ate and mated all the time. Pigeons would be related to the overwhelming passion that adolescents feel.

The young man in the dream was an aspect of Paul's shadow, a *puer aeternus* or eternal boy.[12] This shadow side could not enter a mature relationship and denied the deeper source of love, the goddess. There was potential for life but also for psychological death. The alternately live and dead or dying dove is related to the way Paul experienced his relationships with women.

In the dream there seems to be a possibility for love to come into his life, but the *puer,* Paul's shadow side, has no feeling for it, for what love is. Psychologically this points to a primitive stage of anima development.

D. was the woman Paul was living with, but she was also an inner anima figure appearing in a positive form in previous dreams. She was the human woman who brought the goddess' love into effective earthly contact; that is, she brought Paul down to earth—which of course his shadow *puer* did not like. The lysis of the dream speaks directly to Paul's conscious thoughts about leaving his partner once again. Not only would the inner soul mate lose its vitality and its connection to the goddess of love, the feminine aspect of the Self, but the actual woman would also experience a kind of death.

Young men can bear the loss of the anima without injury, for it is their masculine side of consciousness which must be developed and recognized. But in the second half of life, a new appreciation for feminine nature, both internal and external, must be established in order for a man to be capable of a mature love relationship and also to connect with his inner life.[13] Where there is no sacrifice of immature ego demands or purely collective masculine values, a certain

---

12 See Marie-Louise von Franz, *Puer Aeternus: A Psychological Study of the Adult Struggle with the Paradise of Childhood.*

13 See the section below, "Anima Development in Middle Life."

rigidity sets in, a stoniness toward the joy of life; all that is left is a compelling drive for power or material gain.

Paul's dream indicated a regressive position as it shows no feeling, no remorse for the death of either the goddess as the bringer of divine love, or the human woman, who in this man's psychology would be the equivalent of the sacred prostitute.

Speaking of the anima, Jung notes that "if the unconscious figures are not acknowledged as spontaneous agents, we become victims of a one-sided belief in the power of consciousness."[14] Ruled only by a conscious, masculine position, a man is cut off from his soul. The principle of Eros, the feeling of relatedness, is not operative; consequently, the man remains detached, unable to experience either his own emotions or his spiritual nature.

In such a situation, ego consciousness, in its rational, orderly manner, becomes fortified against what it experiences as the disorienting effect of the feminine:

> Self-control is a typically masculine ideal, to be achieved by the repression of feeling. Feeling is a specifically feminine virtue . . . . A man in trying to attain his ideal of manhood represses all feminine traits—which are really a part of him.[15]

If the ego feels threatened by the other-worldly character of the feminine, there develops a strong defense which results in over-identification with masculine persona roles. These roles may be culturally defined, or related to the mask one wears in professional life. Often a man fails to differentiate between his essential identity and his persona, becoming only the mask.

This was Charles' psychological situation when he first began analysis. He was an ordained minister, skillful in this role and as an administrator. His clerical collar was the emblem with which he identified himself. Publicly he was admired for his capabilities, but he was profoundly lonely. There were perhaps one or two trusted relationships where he allowed his true feelings to show. Moreover, his relationship with himself felt like an endless, hopeless mess.

His presenting concern was a deep hollow feeling and a certain barrenness in his life. His marriage of twenty-five years offered more anxiety than solace; as he approached retirement age, he wondered

---

14 "Commentary on "The Secret of the Golden Flower,"" *Alchemical Studies,* CW 13, par. 62.
15 "Mind and Earth,"*Civilization in Transition,* CW 10, par. 79.

what he would do for the rest of his life if the current superficial connection with his wife continued.

Charles was an educated man in his mid-fifties. He lived a well-ordered life. He had been raised in a rural community amid extended family ruled by his paternal grandfather, a typically patriarchal environment. As was the custom in his family, Charles frequently attended church and revival meetings. Neither family members nor preachers could satisfactorily answer the young man's burning questions about his religious feelings; his personal God was trapped in the strong admonitions of revivalist Old Testament preaching and the patriarchal authority of Church, community and family. The feminine was acceptable only as mother or wife, otherwise she was identified with sex and sin.

The mother-wife, static aspect of Charles' unconscious feminine was evident in his dreams. Dominating consciousness, it prevented any connection to the image of feminine nature as moving, dynamic. Here are two of his dreams during the early stages of analysis:

> My mother and I were in my car going to get fuel. We discussed how far I could travel on one tank, like from this city and back. We were standing behind the car when a couple of guys in an old model car jumped the curb and ran between me and my mother. I tried to scream out Help! Help! but I was too frightened. (I awoke terrified with stiff arms and hands.)

> I was eating dinner with my wife and a female friend. We were seated at a table in a large church convention hall. We were having some conversation but my wife kept cutting me off. I got up and left. . . . We were apart physically and emotionally after the efforts to talk at the table.

Fuel is energy, which psychologically is associated with libido, the psychic energy available for life. The car represents the dreamer's persona, that is, his role as a minister. The beginning of the first dream thus shows Charles' energy and persona tied up with the mother. This refers not to the personal mother, but to the static, elemental feminine, reflecting an attitude toward life that goes with what is safe, guarded and protected. In this case it is also related to Mother Church. The dreamer's fuel or source of energy therefore seems to be derived from the mother-bound component of his psyche.

Two reckless male figures come between mother and son, breaking their strong alliance. As shadow figures they are incompatible with the dreamer's image of himself, yet a potentially healthy eruptive force. Of course, the threatening loss of the dreamer's source of energy, the security of an undisturbed life, is absolutely terrifying; yet at this point in the dreamer's life, it is necessary. It is also significant that there are *two* shadow figures, an example of the doubling motif, which points to something new on the brink of consciousness.[16]

The situation is symbolically similar in the second dream; however, it lacks the redeeming feature of something breaking through. The dreamer feels only estrangement and separation. Now it is the wife aspect of the mother-wife image which prevents communication with the other faces of the feminine. Eating in the church hall—being nourished within the walls of collective Christian thought—points to the dreamer's conventional attitudes. In effect he is in a safe container, but that is the very situation in which he feels cut off, "apart physically and emotionally," from the feminine other.

Along with such mother-wife dreams illustrating an alienation from the full dynamic of the feminine, other dreams indicated a rigid spiritual function. Both kinds of dreams occurred during the same time period.

> I was making a journey with another man to a chapel—the church of my youth. When we got there we had to detour and come from the back due to high water. The water was almost over the road. There was a crust of snow over the edges of the water and vegetation and the churchyard. The flood water was yellow and dingy. We decided there would be no gathering because of the high water.

> I was fishing. I caught no fish but saw large fish frozen in big blocks of ice.

The burning religious quest of Charles' youth was sinking into the high flood waters of the unconscious. The fish, most notable as an early Christian symbol (one often marked at the bottom of the pages in his dream diary) is symbolic of both the Christ image and new life, but here the life is frozen. The icy starkness, empty church, no greenery, no gathering, all point to an absence of life. On the other hand, there is now a male traveling companion; the safe, approving mother attitudes have been replaced by a new, yet unknown, masculine attitude.

---

[16] See Marie-Louise von Franz, *Shadow and Evil in Fairytales,* pp. 31f, and *On Divination and Synchronicity,* pp. 105ff.

Other dreams contained images of the inner feminine as sick, old or bedridden:

> I was with this woman. She was rather undeveloped or slow witted. We had intercourse and during this time it was discovered that she had need of radical female surgery.

> An old hag drives up the hill where I am in a special rigged car so that she can drive. She is very old and very much a hag. I had been friendly to her before but now I am tired of her whiny demands and dependence.

> There is a selection being done for a chaplain. An old woman in bed was conducting it. Several of us to be chosen are gathered around. I went up to her bed to ask if I might say a word.

In these dreams the image of the feminine lacks vitality; sick and disabled feminine figures parallel the inertness of the desolate churchyard and frozen fish. In this comparison we can see the relationship between the feminine and the spiritual. There is nothing to suggest a dynamic feminine presence; however, the dreamer is beginning to be conscious of the demands of his inner woman. He seems to be aware of the power she has over him, yet at the same time wants to be her chosen one.

In time the image of the feminine began to change, as did Charles' attitude toward his persona and his sexuality. The transformation was mirrored in subsequent dreams:

> I was with a young, sexually immature male. I was telling him about his sexual organs and about how to achieve sexual intercourse with women. He or I or we had some type of drink—wine or liquor.

> I was riding in a car with three very attractive girls, with a male driver. One of the girls was talking to me and in a nice way propositioned me. I realized they were prostitutes, and politely refused their offer in that I am a minister. I reached over and touched all three with my hands.

> A tall, well-built, black woman wearing a brown sweater turned into the office in front of me. She asked me, "Who do you kiss?"

> I was lying with a woman. She was hidden from view, but I was fully open to the public. A black woman recognized me as the "Reverend" and began telling me about her grief. Then she realized what was going on and became upset with me; still, she accepted me. Before she left, we embraced each other. I kissed her and a small baby she was holding.

After the dreamer's psychologically immature masculine side (perhaps related to the new traveling companion in the third dream) became open to instruction and they celebrated with the drink of Dionysus, the active feminine could approach ego consciousness. The dreamer, although still in his ministerial persona, is not offended at being propositioned by the prostitutes, and can even reach out to touch these provocative new images of the anima. Then he has an encounter with a black woman, personifying the chthonic feminine— dark, earthy and mysterious.

In the last dream of the series, having become more accepting of his sexuality and now aware that it need not be in conflict with his public image, he could show genuine affection for this earthy side of himself and her child, symbol of his own new life.

The principle of relatedness, antithetical to Charles' earlier patriarchal stance, now had a firm foothold in consciousness, energizing him in a new and exciting way. As the following dreams show, this active principle added an adventurous new dimension to his life, one which could take him to places heretofore unknown.

> I was going up on top of a low building to preach, and a very attractive red-haired girl was going with me. She was to be my soloist. On the way up, I kissed her. She was very responsive and we kissed some more. She suggested we go to her place afterward.

> I was in a boat with a woman (in real life she is a chaplain). We were discussing our appreciation for each other and felt alive sexually with each other. She was driving the boat and I was sitting behind her. We crossed over the main river and stopped on the other bank. She was showing me around. This place was almost like an enchanted land. The houses and people were all very neat.

Charles had arrived at a new psychological place. The active, moving feminine, loving and erotic, was being integrated into consciousness, no longer in conflict with his spiritual side. Moreover, she was leading him into new, unexplored places in his own psyche, the neglected inner world of his emotions.

D.H. Lawrence's *The Man Who Died*

The awe experienced by a man in meeting with his anima—the inner guide who can contain the mysteries of sexuality and spirituality—is illustrated in D. H. Lawrence's short novel, *The Man Who Died.*

It is a story of a wanderer in Jerusalem, a Christ figure who has had a tormented, public life and now seeks something more fulfilling. His situation is analogous to that of many men who in the second half of life feel compelled to turn inward.

As he sets out on his journey with painful, open wounds, he meets a woman who is a priestess of Isis. He says to himself, "This girl of Isis is a tender flame of healing. I am a physician, yet I have no healing like the flame of this tender girl. But dare I come into this tender touch of life? Oh, this is harder."[17]

He is absorbed and enmeshed in new sensations as the woman goes into the shrine and gives herself to the feelings and the urge of Isis. She is lovely to him with the mysterious fire of a potent woman, and he is touched by her desire for him. He trembles with fear and with joy, saying to himself, "I am almost more afraid of this touch than I was of death. For I am more nakedly exposed to it."[18] His wounds begin to cry again, the cry of regret and guilt.

The priestess anoints his scars, saying, "What was torn becomes a new flesh, what was a wound is full of fresh life." He tells her of a woman who once washed his feet and wiped them with her hair, pouring on precious ointment.

[The Priestess asked] "Did you love her?"

"Love had passed in her. She only wanted to serve," he replied. "She had been a prostitute."

"And did you let her serve you?" she asked. . . . "Did you let her serve you with the corpse of her love?" . . .

A vivid shame went through him. "After all," he thought, "I wanted them to love with dead bodies."[19]

The man who died also felt the pain and death inside his own darkness. In this new consciousness, he felt the stir of something coming, a new dawning. "Now I am not myself. I am something new."[20] And he said, "Lo, Isis is a kindly goddess; and full of tenderness. . . . She is dear to me in the middle of my being."[21]

---

17 D.H. Lawrence, *The Man Who Died*, p. 196.

18 Ibid., p. 202.

19 Ibid., p. 204.

20 Ibid., p. 206

21 Ibid., pp. 207f.

This is a moving example of a man meeting the anima in the image of the sacred prostitute, one who is able to mediate between the wounded body of denied instinctual energies and the numinous experience of the divine. Although fearful that his wounded masculine nature would be more exposed and subject to more torment, the man opened himself to the tender healing and beneficial way of the priestess of Isis.

Here the sacred prostitute, as one aspect of the anima, functions as mediatrix between consciousness and the unconscious, bringing instinctual forces into harmony with the divine. Without an appreciation of this image, contemporary man experiences a major split between the spiritual and sensual aspects of Eros. Sexual acts devoid of an attitude of tribute to the goddess become merely instinctual performances without connection to the inner being.

Many modern men experience this split. "Man cannot come to a positive connection to his anima until this split is reconciled and healed," writes Robert Stein.[22] Conversely, it may be that this split cannot be healed until a man has found a positive connection to his anima. What is necessary in a man's psychological development is for him to experience the transformative, active side of the anima. Only then can he abandon conventional, constricted attitudes toward the feminine and enter into the world of full emotional involvement with another.

Stages of the Anima

As a man's consciousness widens, his attitude toward both his own feminine side and women in general is altered. Jung describes four stages of anima development, analogous to historical images of the feminine personified by Eve, Helen of Troy, the Virgin Mary and Sophia:

> The first stage—Hawwah, Eve, earth—is purely biological; woman is equated with mother and only represents something to be fertilized. The second stage is still dominated by the sexual Eros, but on the aesthetic and romantic level where woman has already acquired some value as an individual. The third stage raises Eros to the heights of religious devotion and thus spiritualizes him: Hawwah has been replaced by spiritual motherhood. Finally, the fourth stage

---

[22] Robert Stein, "The Animus and Impersonal Sexuality," in *Spring 1970*, p. 126.

illustrates something which unexpectedly goes beyond the almost unsurpassable third stage: *Sapientia* [Sophia]. . . . This stage represents a spiritualization of Helen and consequently of Eros as such. That is why *Sapientia* was regarded as a parallel to the Shulamite in the Song of Songs.[23]

At first glance, Jung's description of anima figures in their progressive stages seems restrictive, as if to imply that only when the anima advances out of the instinctive stage, negating sexual feelings, can one develop spiritually. We ask ourselves whether this is yet another echo of the morality of our culture where sexuality is considered the antithesis of spirituality. If we interpret it in this way, "small wonder then that a wild and confusing conflict arises between man as an instinctual creature of nature and man as a spiritually conditioned cultural being."[24]

A more careful consideration of the passage, however, suggests that Jung is actually emphasizing the presence of Eros, in its broadest sense, at every stage of anima development. Elsewhere he writes, "Sexuality is not mere instinctuality; it is an indisputably creative power that is not only the basic cause of our individual lives, but a very serious factor in our psychic life as well."[25]

At the apex of the anima's development, then, her spiritual aspect encompasses her sexuality. It is contained in the very nature of Sapientia (Sophia), who was the bride of God. In the Bible she says, "I was daily his delight, rejoicing always before him; Rejoicing in the habitable part of his earth; and my delights were with the sons of men."[26] According to an alchemical text, the *Rosarium philosophorum*, "On her robe is written in gold lettering . . . I am the only daughter of the wise, utterly unknown to the foolish."[27]

The erotic nature of the highest order of the anima is also seen in the image of the Shulamite, and through this image we find a connection to the sacred prostitute. The Shulamite was a priestess of

---

23 "The Psychology of the Transference," *The Practice of Psychotherapy*, CW 16, par. 361.

24 Jung, Introduction to Esther Harding, *The Way of All Women*, p. xviii.

25 "On Psychic Energy," *The Structure and Dynamics of the Psyche*, CW 8, par. 107.

26 Proverbs 8:30-31.

27 Quoted by Jung in "Religious Ideas in Alchemy," *Psychology and Alchemy*, CW 12, par. 467.

Ishtar; Jung says that she signifies "earth, nature, fertility, everything that flourishes under the damp light of the moon, and also the natural life-urge."[28]

The sacred prostitute, then, while not synonymous with the anima, is a feminine image relevant to every stage of development of man's inner woman. She offers pleasure, excitement and vitality, a personification of both spirituality and earthiness. She is a lover whose beauty is exciting, whose virginal nature brings forth new life and leads to Wisdom—which is more than simply intellect.

Each successive stage of the anima brings new realizations and an altering of attitudes; at the same time, paradoxically, the influence of the preceding stage is not diminished but rather enhanced. Initially, as Eve, the sacred prostitute is in tune with her biological, sexual nature. She desires physical pleasure. In her wantonness, she desires not *the* man but *a* man. She is not only the giver of sexual pleasure but the receiver. She is matter and body and earth.

As Helen, whose beauty and charm have been idealized as a prototype of erotic love though the ages,[29] the sacred prostitute has these same attributes. She is the beautiful one whose dress and perfume, whose awareness of her rounded form in the movements of her dancing, charms the male and excites his passion. At this stage of anima development, she is seen as more than body—she is an individual in her own right, experienced as the feminine Other. She takes on a particular personality.

The sacred prostitute also has certain characteristics in common with the Virgin Mary, although this is difficult to comprehend because our current cultural image of Mary is clouded by a foggy notion of purity and piety. That is the effect of the split between the sexual and the holy. But there is another image of Mary—as a "black" madonna—which contains and appreciates these apparently contradictory concepts.[30] Like Mary, the sacred prostitute is considered virginal (psychologically); just as Mary's virginal womb brought forth the Christ child, so does the womb of the sacred prostitute, as anima, give birth to man's Christ-like nature, his higher consciousness.

---

28 "Adam and Eve," *Mysterium Coniunctionis,* CW 14, par. 646.

29 "All is dross that is not Helen."—Marlowe.

30 The image of the black madonna is discussed below, in chapter 5.

In Roman Catholic tradition, Mary is seen as the intercessor between God and man, leading man to God to assure his immortality. In a similar manner, it was the sacred prostitute who, in welcoming the male into her sacred room and entering into the worship of the deity, was the intercessor, the mediatrix, between the deity and man. The inner woman, through various developmental stages, performs the same function as the mediatrix, notably in the act of sexual love where the physical and personal are transcended.

As described above, Sophia (Sapientia/the Shulamite) parallels aspects of the anima, yet she should also be considered as an aspect of the divine being, analogous to the archetype of the Self.[31] Sophia is Wisdom. In Biblical tradition she is both the bride of God and the mother, the lover who was with God before Creation.[32] She is the feminine being who is "a friend and playmate from the beginning of the world, the first born of all God's creatures, a stainless reflection of his glory and a master workman."[33] Jung quotes from the Wisdom of Solomon to describe her:

> She is "the breath of the power of God," "a pure effluence flowing from the glory of the Almighty," "The brightness of the everlasting light, the unspotted mirror of the power of God," a being "most subtil" who "passeth and goeth through all things by reason of her pureness." She is "conversant with God," and "the Lord of all things himself loved her." . . . She is sent from heaven and from the throne of glory as a "Holy Spirit."[34]

We have seen earlier that the sacred prostitute, in the celebration of the sacred marriage, embodied the goddess and was identified with her. She was the bride of God, represented by the king. In the union of the sacred marriage, she brought the regenerative power of Wisdom into effective contact with the lives of men.

In each of these stages a man becomes aware of a different aspect of his own feminine nature. He is led, as it were, by one anima image or another through life's experiences. Ideally, on his path of individuation, he will come to incorporate the full continuum of his in-

---

[31] Jung, "The Psychology of the Transference," *The Practice of Psychotherapy,* CW 16, par. 518.

[32] Proverbs 8:23-30.

[33] Jung, "Answer to Job," *Psychology and Religion: West and East,* CW 11, par. 617.

[34] Ibid., par. 613.

Sophia/Sapientia/Wisdom.
(Italian manuscript, medieval; Vatican Library)

stinctive energies and his spiritual essence, an experience that culminates in the *hieros gamos,* the sacred marriage or uniting of the opposites.[35] Such a man enters into the sexual act not from a desire for power or the need to control, but with a feeling of honor for, and devotion to, the mystery of the feminine.

In this affective contact with the anima, invariably mirrored in his relationships with actual women, masculine ego consciousness attains an essential enlightenment. Like the stranger who entered the temple of love, a man gives up an aspect of ego consciousness in order to join with the Other. This union itself symbolizes the equality of male and female; neither is dominating, demanding or possessing. Through this positive relationship with the anima a man experiences an exciting, moving vitality in his life; old ideas and values which have become burdensome are lifted from his shoulders.

Yet this new consciousness is not achieved without frustration, conscious suffering and fear, for it is invariably accompanied by disconcerting changes.

Anima Development in Middle Life

Discontent, boredom and a general lack of enthusiasm are common symptoms of an anima problem, especially in the second half of life. If a man experiences the feminine only as the maternal—and therefore as something to be fertilized or feared—can the transformative influence of the sacred prostitute be realized? The endless sameness of a comfortable and predictable relationship is often the Scylla and Charybdis which provokes the inner search for, and development of, the anima.

Such was the case with John, a man in his mid-forties. He spoke of deep dissatisfaction with his life; he lacked energy and interest both at home and at work. He was an extremely hard worker, but he did not view his work as successful and was very pessimistic because of frequent setbacks. This pessimism was also reflected in his marriage of eighteen years, for he felt that all he did was to no avail. Most often he felt a morbid resignation to his "unhappy fate," yet on occasion there was a glimmer of hope that his life might be different.

---

[35] See "On the Nature of the Psyche," *The Structure and Dynamics of the Psyche,* CW 8, pars. 413-414, where Jung uses the simile of the spectrum to explain the synthesis of conscious and unconscious contents, symbolized by the sacred marriage.

As his analyst, I initially experienced John as rigid and obstinate, clutching old values in an inflexible way. He had a growing need for alcohol, which on several occasions had resulted in drunkenness. This in turn created guilt, remorse and depression. Such symptoms are among those described by Jung as indicative of the need to make contact with the anima.

> After the middle of life . . . loss of the anima means a diminution of vitality, of flexibility, and of human kindness. The result, as a rule, is premature rigidity, crustiness, stereotypy, fanatical one-sidedness, obstinacy, pedantry, or else resignation, weariness, sloppiness, irresponsibility, and finally a childish *ramollissement* [lethargy] with a tendency to alcohol. After middle life, therefore, the connection with the archetypal sphere of experience should if possible be re-established.[36]

Jung also pointed out the similarity between the concept of "loss of soul" among primitives and what happens to a man who loses contact with his anima:

> Loss of soul amounts to a tearing loose of part of one's nature; it is the disappearance and emancipation of a complex, which thereupon becomes a tyrannical usurper of consciousness, oppressing the whole man. It throws him off course and drives him to actions whose blind one-sidedness inevitably leads to self-destruction.[37]

So it was with John, for there was a strong masculine ego and considerable conscious development but little recognition of the earthy, irrational feminine base of the unconscious.

Early in the analytic process the anima began to present herself, as in the following dream:

> I was at a farm, in a pasture, and decide to carry a gun and hunt. There were some buildings of a school-type. My wife was there but all the others were very conventional, even "goody-goody" type men. I carried a pint of whisky in my hand but felt uncomfortable so I put it in my pocket. There was a round storage bin for grain. I go into it but it is below ground level. A girl is there whose name is Lola. She is a whore. I wanted to make love to her but when I started she said, "I don't do that," but I knew she did and we did. Several men stopped by, one from the power company and one from the

---

[36] "Concerning the Archetypes and the Anima Concept,"*The Archetypes and the Collective Unconscious,* CW 9i, par. 147.

[37] "The Type Problem in Poetry," *Psychological Types,* CW 6, par. 384.

conservation department. We did not finish the act and I awoke frustrated and unfulfilled.

The open pastures belong to the Earth Mother, and here is where the dream-ego seeks the female (in the vernacular, goes "hunting") with phallic symbol in hand. This presents an image of a rugged outdoor-type man, a shadow side of John not often apparent in his gentlemanly manners. John's persona was in fact related to the "school-type buildings" in the dream: rational, intellectualizing and conservative. This was the image with which he identified (and apparently the one his wife saw and supported). The "goody-goody" side of himself is apparently not compatible with his strong, erotic "hunter" nature, which was repressed and therefore consciously incongruous to John. The whiskey-from-the-bottle aspect of the shadow was in fact being acted out in bouts of drinking.

In John's associations to the dream, he related that in his youth he had known a girl named Lola who had been a prostitute. He described her as "wily but clean." He also thought of the musical, *Damn Yankees,* in which the female lead, Lola, is a beautiful woman in league with the devil. She sings a song, "Whatever Lola wants, Lola gets." Another association was that his wife was a school teacher, and that there was a striking difference between the two dream women, wife and whore.

The storage grain bin where the girl is found is related to Demeter and the Kore (Persephone)—Demeter, the maternal image associated with grain, and the Kore, Demeter's daughter, who was abducted by Hades, the devil. Here the dream-ego (John's hunter shadow) finds Lola (the dynamic aspect of the feminine, his own inner Kore) "below ground level," which psychologically points to her being contained in the maternal womb of the unconscious. Lola is undifferentiated woman, an object to be used. The sexual act is like a rape, since Lola does not enter into it freely. For a man to take a woman more or less by force, not honoring her "no," is indicative of a primitive sexual attitude, which here, apparently, is a characteristic of John's shadow.[38]

The men from the "power company" and the "conservation department" are analogous to those self-regulatory psychic compo-

---

[38] It is true that a woman might say "no" ambivalently, both fearing and desiring the penetration of the masculine. However, this fine distinction is for the woman to reflect on; it does not justify intercourse without consent.

nents which monitor the flow of psychic energy—libido—and warn against the misuse of natural resources. The sexual act was entered into for instant self-gratification, with no respect for the "otherness" of the woman or for the goddess of love. The appearance of the men and their interruption of the sex act leaves the dreamer feeling frustrated and unfulfilled.

This dream troubled John and led him to wrestle consciously with his shadow side and repressed attitudes toward the feminine, which held his anima at the Eve stage—like a young girl still closely connected with the mother. The image of the feminine as prostitute is promising, but at this point she is simply used by the shadow and there is no sense of the sacred.

In struggling with his shadow, John also became conscious of hostility and even fear toward woman. Again this side of himself was so incompatible with his conscious self-image that it had been repressed. Using the technique of active imagination, he became friends with his inner Lola, who at one point said to him, "You didn't love me enough." On one occasion he had a compelling urge to play music for her, as if to create a feeling of harmony between them.

Gradually there was a transformation in John's conscious attitudes, as reflected in the following dream.

> I was looking for calves up on a hill. I came to an old house and went in. There were four or five women there. A young girl was sitting at a reception desk and another one was behind her. We talked and I brushed my lips against hers. The second girl whispered she wanted me to go with her. I followed her through several rooms. She was nude and absolutely breathtakingly beautiful. We came to another room with straw on the floor as in a loft. My feeling was she was a bitch and a lover in one.

"Looking for calves" indicates John's growing awareness of the love goddess, who as mentioned earlier was often imaged with a crescent-moon headdress, related to cow horns. The calves, an image or representation of the "newly born" goddess, must be found. This search leads the dreamer to the house of women.

The house in the dream is reminiscent of a brothel; the fact that it is old may point to the dreamer's outdated collective attitudes toward sex and women. But because of the erotic atmosphere it may also indicate a growing differentiation in his personal attitude toward the feminine, a movement toward seeing and appreciating them as sexual beings.

Often when a man dreams of several women, one comes forward and presents herself; she holds a special quality and is particularly attracted to the dream-ego. Here such a woman becomes the dream-ego's guide through an unknown labyrinth. This alluring and charming woman is receptive to his masculine potency; she is neither overwhelmed nor forced as in the previous dream. There is a humble and unpretentious atmosphere, denoted by the straw on the floor. John is still ambivalent, perceiving the woman in the dream as both bitch and lover. At the same time, he is fascinated by her beauty, charm and promise of love.

The dream depicts the beginning of the Helen stage of anima development, which manifests through John's efforts to seek an inner connection to the love goddess. Fascinated, he follows her into the unknown places of the feminine realm. Now he shows a certain respect—he is awe-struck by her sheer beauty, an attitude quite different from that in the earlier dream, where the masculine had the "right" to ravish the feminine.

The anima now becomes more receptive, more accessible. Here we find a strong parallel with the stranger who seeks to honor the goddess; John comes to the sacred prostitute and is welcomed by her. She, in being receptive to the masculine, brings the dreamer to a new acknowledgment of the Other, his own inner woman.

In John's outer reality, he was experiencing much confusion; as he expressed it, "my world is turning upside down." As new psychic elements began to be known, others were in a stage of transformation; naturally there was a sense of disorientation. The crusty barnacles of old attitudes were slowly dissolving, while only fragile outlines of new ones had formed. Yet even within this chaos, John was accepting new dimensions of life in which he felt a certain excitement and exhilaration. There was an unwonted courage, far from his former resignation, to pursue new avenues of self-expression in writing and music, and the rediscovery of classical literature, thereby balancing his overzealous attachment to work.

Several months later another dream showed the further development of the anima:

> I was at a church service and was sitting between two older obese women. I go to take communion and the two celebrants were women dressed in white. One has the host which is wrapped in silver. She asks if I want to look at it or will I have it. I tell her I will have it.

The other has the chalice but she hits it against my forehead and wine spills on my head like a baptism. I go back to my seat and there an attractive blonde is sitting next to me. I do not think it is my proper place and move back between the two older women. Now I feel squeezed and move back to the girl. As I go toward her, she stands up and walks toward me. She has a big lump on the left side of her head which I had not noticed before. It is a third eye. I was shocked by that.

The two older, obese women suggest the static, maternal aspect of the feminine, which continues to color John's attitude toward women in outer reality; however, now he is willing to approach the altar, the place where ego demands and old attitudes are sacrificed. In doing so he is freed from the maternal influence.

At the time of the dream, women had not yet been ordained as priests in the church John attended, therefore the priestesses here are archetypal elements emerging spontaneously from the unconscious. The priestesses stand before the altar, the sacred precinct—as did the sacred prostitute—to offer the Eucharist, the sacrificial elements for the strengthening and renewal of life. The dreamer does not enter into the service vicariously, just by looking, but is receptive to emotional and spiritual involvement with the divine.

The host wrapped in silver, the metal of the moon and therefore of the goddess, is symbolic of body or matter. The chalice, associated with the Holy Grail, is the feminine vessel containing the essential soul substance from which the spirit emanates. The baptism of wine, symbolic of blood, is associated with ancient rites of passage during which the initiate was covered or marked with the blood of the sacrificial animal. Wine is also associated with the ecstatic worship of the god Dionysus by his women followers. It was considered the inspiriting drink of divine ecstasy.

By participating in this ecstatic religious experience, ingesting or internalizing the symbolic form of matter or sensuality, and being bathed in the renewing spiritual element, the dreamer is led to a new position. After communion with the priestesses, he cannot return to his previous orientation but finds a new image of the feminine—the moving, transformative aspect of the anima who comes forward to meet him.

Both the priestess and the attractive blonde are images of the sacred prostitute, although they appear to be different, just as the sacred prostitute when she stood before the altar did not appear the same as when she was in her sacred chamber. The third eye is an archetypal image of wisdom and insight into the spiritual mysteries. It is quite the opposite of the rational intellect, which was John's forte and on which he automatically relied.

Jung writes of the Eucharist as a symbol of the individuation process.[39] It is reminiscent of the ancient new moon festival, dedicated to the goddess, where moon cakes and libations of blood were served to restrengthen life. In the role of mediatrix, also the role of the sacred prostitute, the priestess is ministrant of the sacraments. She mediates between the deity and man by offering the symbolic elements of both body and spirit. This development of the anima parallels that of the role of the Virgin Mary as mediatrix between earthly man and God. This anima image embodies the profound spiritual essence of feminine nature.

The dreamer now becomes aware of an inner feminine image that is woman but more than human. This touches the facets of the feminine aspect of the Self, the highest expression of wisdom. Her "third eye" brings illuminating insight rather than abstract or fragmented knowledge. Hers is a responsive wisdom which comes from a loving connection with the divine.

Near the end of the analysis, John had the following dream.

> I am in a green farm house. There are phonograph records on the bed. Several were broken records and had been taped together and I thought how can anyone play those and threw them away. Then I leave and enter into a large crowd. It is a wedding party and it is to be my wedding. I don't know anyone in the wedding party. Now across the street, I am preparing for my wedding. I notice my shoes are not appropriate and I wonder about them but then I realize I have a new pair and those will be fine.

Green is the color of spring, of new life, and also the color associated with the goddess. In her shelter (which is now above ground, thus more conscious as compared to its underground location in the first dream), the initial preparations for the sacred marriage take place. This involves discarding old collective attitudes, which like broken records are no longer useful. The bed is where dream life is activated, thus a place where one becomes more intimate with one's unconscious.

---

[39] "Transformation Symbolism in the Mass," *Psychology and Religion: West and East,* CW 11, pars. 296ff.

Now the dreamer must leave the green house, the sphere of the earth goddess, in order to arrive at a new dimension, that of uniting with—integrating—more developed aspects of the feminine. The bride-to-be, whose features are as yet unknown, may be thought of as the more human aspect of the goddess. This parallels the ritual marriage of ancient times where the sacred prostitute, as the incarnation of the goddess, was the bride.

For this inner marriage, the dreamer's shoes, related to his standpoint in life, are not appropriate. However, the dream ends with the reassurance that a new standpoint is available. This realization portends a fresh conscious attitude grounded in a new awareness of the feminine. The next step in the dreamer's process of individuation would be to proceed to the sacred *temenos,* the chamber where the opposites are united in the sacred marriage, where feminine nature is truly integrated with the masculine principle.

This example of one man's encounter with the Other demonstrates the developmental stages of the anima in which a man's inner feminine nature is made conscious, accepted and honored. Typically, as happened in John's case, such a process is accompanied by a significant change in the man's external relationships with women and in his general outlook on life. Contact with the dynamic aspect of the anima has a transforming effect, bringing a sense of joy and humor and suffusing the personality with a noticeable enthusiasm.

In Goethe's *Faust,* one sees a similar transformation of the anima as she changes from Gretchen to Helen, and finally to the Mother of God. As Jung points out, Faust's nature "is altered by repeated figurative deaths" until he attains the highest state of consciousness represented by Dr. Marianus.[40]

Indeed, John experienced considerable suffering through the "death" of those rigid, collective attitudes which stress an orientation toward material values and deny the inner reality of the feminine. Yet this death was also his offering, the sacrifice of known values, of outer stability and maternal comfort. He came as a wounded man with open psychic sores—as a stranger to the unknown place. There he met the anima in her various guises. She guided him through the neglected inner world of emotions, of Eros and ecstasy. She taught him to feel the harmonic rhythm of life's forces; she was the mediator

---

[40] "The Type Problem in Poetry," *Psychological Types,* CW 6, par. 378.

between the sensual and the spiritual aspects of his life, both of which had for many years been neglected and repressed.

*

To summarize, the sacred prostitute in masculine psychology corresponds to an aspect of the anima that functions as a moving and transforming psychic force. She is directly related to a man's conscious understanding and integration of his own contrasexual nature. She modifies a man's self-image, conscious values and attitude toward women in outer life.

The sacred prostitute aspect of the anima brings joy and laughter and enables the man to see beauty and to feel the emotions of love. As a soul-image connected with the goddess of love, the divine feminine aspect of a man's Self, she transforms instinctive sexual expression into *love-making*, an exhilarating experience that is in no way incompatible with his spiritual nature.

In our modern world, the image of the sacred prostitute is buried under the religious, political and economic values of the patriarchy. She lives still, however, and may be rediscovered as a soul-mate by any man with the will and courage to sacrifice stereotypical masculine persona roles and outdated collective values. They are the offering he brings to the sacred prostitute in the temple of love; there she waits, ready to initiate him into the meaning of his life and awaken his consciousness to a new wisdom.

Left, Venus of Willendorf.—Limestone, paleolithic, Austria.
(Naturhistorisches Museum, Vienna)

Right, Venus of Menton.—Soapstone, paleolithic, France.
(Musée des antiquités nationales, St-Germaine-en-Laye)

4

The Sacred Prostitute
in Feminine Psychology

When he prepared the heavens, I was there . . . .
Then I was by him, as one brought up with him: and I
was daily his delight, rejoicing always before him.
—The Voice of Wisdom, Proverbs 8: 27, 30.

Introduction

As early as the Neolithic Age, images of women were fashioned from
stone, bone or clay, with corpulent hips, a full belly ripe with new
life and enormous breasts rich with nourishment. Two famous relics
from these early times are shown opposite. Such figures represented
Mother Earth who contained the mystery of regenerating life.[1] Yet
there was little differentiation in this portrayal of abundance, as
shown in the lack of facial features, hands and feet.

As civilization developed, Mother Earth ceased to be singularly
identified with fertility and became associated also with the goddess
of love and passion. Then the artist's eye beheld an additional kind of
beauty in the feminine form. The delicate features of Botticelli's *Birth
of Venus,* for example, or the series of the provocative Venus painted
by Cranach, depict the symmetry and proportions of the elegant,
unashamedly sensuous feminine body. Graceful feet and hands with
slender, tapering fingers and an animated face characterize the image
of the goddess of love created by artists in the form of human
woman. In addition to physical beauty, these images reflected a
peaceful frame of mind and calm integrity.

Through this archetypal image, the sensuous figure of the goddess
of love, an individual woman becomes aware of her divine feminine
nature. Her human nature, based on attributes of the goddess per-

---

[1] Jung, "The Psychological Aspects of the Kore," *The Archetypes and the
Collective Unconscious,* CW 9i, par. 312.

117

sonified in the sacred prostitute, can then come into a responsible and valid relationship with that divine aspect.

Maintaining the right relationship with the goddess is not an easy endeavor. The history of humankind's attitude to the goddess has left its mark on the psyche of women today. In ancient times the goddess was "venerated."[2] Later, as mentioned in chapter 1, changes in religious tradition resulted in the loss of reverence toward the goddess and the sacred prostitutes who were her priestesses. With the advent of patriarchal religion and the consequent loss of reverence for the goddess, woman's conscious development was considerably hindered. Slowly she came to worship gods made by men; men's values became her values; men's attitudes, justifying the subordination of women, became her attitudes.

Obliterated along with the goddess was the concept of woman as "one-in-herself," a person of integrity;[3] woman defined herself exclusively in terms of her relation to man. She defined her chastity by echoing the masculine, rational, physical criteria, as prescribed by the laws of men, while negating the chastity of her soul.[4] Although this ran counter to her inner feminine core, woman saw herself as inferior, a role she accepted until only recent times.

The loss of the relationship to the goddess has given rise to discontent; without a conscious awareness of her, the ways in which a woman may express her instinctive nature are extremely limited. Women must rediscover the significance of the goddess so that the dynamic aspect of the image, acting as a pattern of behavior, may have an active role in shaping, regulating and motivating feminine consciousness. Jung maintains that

> the realization and assimilation of instinct never take place . . . by absorption into the instinctual sphere, but only through integration of the image which signifies and at the same time evokes the instinct although in a form quite different from the one we meet on the biological level.[5]

---

[2] The word "venerate" stems from the Latin *venerari,* meaning to worship or to reverence. It has the root of *veneris,* meaning love, sexual desire and loveliness, from which the name Venus is derived.

[3] See above, p. 59.

[4] John Layard, *The Virgin Archetype,* p. 291.

[5] "On the Nature of the Psyche," *The Structure and Dynamics of the Psyche,* CW 8, par. 417.

The image of the goddess, associated with the physical beauty of the feminine body, activates archetypal energies pertaining to love, passion and relatedness. The woman who honors these feelings comes to understand and appreciate the sacred prostitute incarnate in her own personality.

The difference between the psychologically immature female (the maiden) and the psychologically mature woman (regardless of age) is that the former would have love serve her, while the latter chooses to serve love, that is, the goddess. Biological sexual instincts are used in such a manner as to honor the Self, not for power or personal gratification. The passion of the sexual act can then be experienced as both physical and spiritual.

A woman's continual denial of the body and her sexuality results in the ossification of mental attitudes contradictory to her potentially "virginal" nature. A little-known myth illustrates this. It tells of a small town, Amathonte, on the island of Cyprus where the women were modest, reserved and contemptuous of all carnal pleasures. They were disdainful of their bodies and covered themselves in a most unattractive manner.

One day, Venus came to their shore and as the women came down to see her, they noticed her nudity and treated her with scorn. So Venus gathered them together and ordered them to make love to all comers so that they might glory in the very flesh they had so disdained. The women had no recourse but to do as she commanded; still, they did it so reluctantly and with such distaste as to defeat the purpose of the goddess. Then Venus came again and punished these women by turning them into stone.[6]

Consciousness of feminine nature begins in deep appreciation of, and caring devotion to, the body. Whatever a woman's shape or size, her body is unique to her and therefore special. Yet the majority of women are caught in the web of propaganda stemming from the world of slick consumerism.

Comparing oneself to others, instead of appreciating what one is, creates a situation in which the inner voice of the negative animus can sneak in with proclamations such as, "You can't measure up! You'll never be good (pretty, desirable, etc.) enough!" All the while the woman is held captive to what she mistakenly identifies as her personal shortcomings.

---

6 B. F. Goldberg, *The Sacred Fire: The Story of Sex in Religion,* p. 91.

Jane, Mary and Susan: Three Single Women

The unconscious attitude toward the body is often revealed in dreams, as in the following examples of three women, each over thirty-five, unmarried and sexually uninitiated.

Two of the women had never had any sexual relationships, while the third was very active sexually but without any feelings of love. (Both abstinence and promiscuity deny the goddess her due.) Each had a well-developed intellectual side but each had neglected, indeed rejected, the body and sexuality as it relates to the goddess.

Here are three of Jane's early dreams:

I am paralyzed from the waist down and talking to someone about planning how to live the rest of my life in a wheelchair.

An image of seeing myself in the mirror—I am in wonder to see that I have a hole in the center of my chest. It is a concave depression.

I am in the hospital because something is the matter with my arms. I have arms like a rag-doll, loose and stuffed with cotton.

It is clear from these that the dreamer is suffering the crippling effect of being cut off from sensual feelings. She has no way of standing firm in her feminine nature. Her arms are simply appendages with no capacity to hold or embrace. The place on her chest where her heart should be has caved in. Jane slowly began to realize that the unconscious was relaying an important message.

After frequent bouts of illness, Jane finally became attentive to the body and its needs. This required that she recognize her unconscious denial of her femininity.

The need for such "clean-up" jobs is often pictured in dreams of dirty bathrooms or overflowing toilets, as in the following:

In the bathroom. I flush the john but it begins to overflow. I get a plumber's helper and that fixes the problem, but a lot of excrement has already overflowed on the floor and I begin to clean it up, which is not only messy and disgusting but also difficult. The damn light bulb has even burned out so it's hard to see and I'm angry at mother because I know she knew the light was out but she didn't do anything about it.

As this dream suggests, Jane's task was all the more difficult because her mother had not given her an adequate understanding of feminine sexuality; she had not provided a "light" in Jane's formative years. Menarche and subsequent menstruation were for Jane hidden and "nightmarish times." No rituals or intimate discussions with an older woman had assisted her in the transition to womanhood.

The rejection of a woman's instinctive nature is of course not always due to the negative influence of the personal mother. In Mary's case, the rigid instruction of the Church and parochial schools had taught that sexuality was only for the purpose of procreation—otherwise it was considered shameful. Mary had come from a large family and was close to the animals on the farm where she lived. She was knowledgeable about instinctive life, but rejected any sexual expression of it. She suffered from an idealistic religious attitude and was fearful of life.

When Mary was in her early thirties she went to live at a convent in preparation to become a nun. She left when she realized that she did want marriage and children, but then followed other religious cults, looking for meaning. She felt herself to be a rather drab person lacking in deeply-felt emotions and living a colorless existence. Early in analysis she had the following dream:

> I am naked sitting with my legs open. My cat comes over to me and begins sniffing me. She goes up between my legs, puts her tongue out and starts to lick my vulva. When she touches me it is as if her tongue is paralyzed or contaminated—she can't put it back into her mouth. It just stays stuck out. I feel so terrible and ashamed that I've allowed this to happen.

Cats, independent and self-assured, have long been associated with instinctive feminine nature. Mythologically, the cat is a symbol for enjoyment and gaiety, as shown in the celebrations mounted for the Egyptian cat goddess Bastet.[7] It could be considered the exact opposite of existential fear.[8] The dreamer's attitude toward her vulva, her sexuality, is not a healthy one and results in the contamination

---

[7] See *New Larousse Encyclopedia of Mythology*, p. 37: "The devout came in hundreds of thousands from all over the country . . . . The journey took place by barges to the sound of flutes and castanets. . . . On the appointed day a splendid procession wound through the town and festivities followed during which, it seems, more wine was drunk than during all the rest of the year."

[8] Marie-Louise von Franz, *Problems of the Feminine in Fairytales*, p. 186: "People who suffer from such fear should cultivate the idea that they are conferring an honour on others by coming into a room and 'letting themselves be stroked.' "

of her true instinctive nature. How opposite is the goddess Inanna's song:

> My vulva, the horn,
> The Boat of Heaven,
> Is full of eagerness like the young moon.
> My untilled land lies fallow.
>
> As for me, Inanna,
> Who will plow my vulva?
> Who will plow my high field?
> Who will plow my wet ground?

Dumuzi answers:

> Great Lady, the king will plow your vulva.
> I, Dumuzi the King, will plow your vulva.

To which Inanna responds:

> Then plow my vulva, man of my heart!
> Plow my vulva![9]

As a woman grows more conscious of her repressed sexuality and feelings, the next step, as noted above, is cleaning up the problem. Mary, like Jane, had a series of bathroom dreams in which she was confronted with her own excrement, annoyed by its smell and unsuccessful in her attempts to hide it. Unpleasant as this might seem, it was the necessary prelude to claiming her feminine nature.

Perhaps the most damaging effects on feminine nature originate in sexual abuse by a familiar adult male, often the father or an older brother. Such acts of violation inflict severe psychic wounds on the budding feminine nature and inhibit a connection to the Self. How can the child grow to love her body, the concretization of her femininity, when it is not respected by the very people she views as "authority?" In order to deal with the psychic pain of invasion the child becomes disassociated from her sexuality.

This was Susan's experience in childhood. Her older brother forced her into frequent sexual acts, beginning at the age of seven and continuing into adolescence. Her mother ignored this and frequently left them alone. The father was an alcoholic whose ranting and raving were equally terrifying. Nowhere did the child feel secu-

---

9 Diane Wolkstein and S. N. Kramer, *Inanna: Queen of Heaven and Earth*, p. 37.

Dumuzi and Inanna.—Clay plaque, ca. 2000 B.C.
(Basel, Erlenmeyer Collection)

rity for herself or her younger sister, whom she carefully protected by taking the abuse upon herself.

Susan also lived on a farm, amid a great deal of poverty. Perhaps there was one saving bit of emotional health, for she remarked that during childhood she often went to be with the cow and said her prayers to her. Only at the deepest levels of the psyche did the archetypal image of the nourishing mother retain some spark of life.

Susan was a beautiful woman, extremely bright and talented. With enormous effort she educated herself and achieved a very responsible position, but not without great cost to her body and her self-image. At one point she took money for sex, and thereafter continued to see herself as a whore. Susan dated often, but without any feelings of love or joy, although she expertly acted these emotions. In her sense of unworthiness, she overcompensated by "performing," as she said, in an extra-witty, extra-charming and extra-exciting way—all counterproductive for the development of her true feminine nature.

Relationships were strictly for the purpose of ego-aggrandizement. "When meeting someone new," she said, "I immediately get out my calculator." She readily gave herself to a man after an expensive evening because, she reasoned, it was expected of her. That was what a prostitute should do.

When Susan came into analysis, her denial of the body was complete. "I've been dead a long time," she said on her initial visit. She had suicidal thoughts; she no longer cared to live a life of self-deprecation, full of depression and extreme loneliness. The isolation was absolute, for nowhere was there more than a superficial connection with another person, nor was there any connection to her feminine core.

Each month Susan suffered from dysmenorrhea. Her physical symptoms were symbolic of her lack of appreciation for her body and for her sexual nature. An early dream showed the severity of her situation:

> I was in the house where I used to baby-sit. The girl who had been the baby sitter before me had committed suicide by throwing herself in the fireplace. The wind came and blew out the ashes and I had to sweep "her" up, bones and everything.

Susan had supported herself in early adolescence by baby-sitting. At that time of change in her maturing body, enraged at her brother's brutal incestuous acts, she had in effect killed off the instinctual part of herself. The passionate potential of youth turned to ashes. The wind, symbol of the pneuma or spirit, brings this out into the open to be cleaned up. The problem here was not simply the recovery of repressed sexual material, as represented in the bathroom dreams of Jane and Mary, but involved reconstituting the dismembered body itself, the burnt bones of her feminine core.

Rejection of one's feminine nature, with an accompanying lack of reverence toward the body, allows the negative animus to acquire tremendous psychic power. He undercuts a woman's sense of beauty, her self-confidence and motivation to be creative. She is his prisoner. In dreams she is trapped, taunted and tortured by this malevolent psychic factor, much as in the light of day she is held captive by a feeling of worthlessness:

> *Jane's dream:* Riding along in a car with mother driving. I'm annoyed with her. The countryside is desolate—looks like craters on the moon—reddish brown, dead. There is a billboard that shows the absence of the TV Indian—the earth has fulfilled his warning.
>
> Then I'm in the back seat of a car. In the front seat are three black males. I look at them and know that they are thugs—really cruel. The one on the right reaches back and locks the door on my side of the car. I am terrified and helpless.
>
> *Mary's dream:* There was a man near my car and I didn't feel good about him being there; but there were several other people in the vicinity, so I just went on to open the car door. As I put my hand on my front door, the man grabbed me. And I start yelling, "Let go! Let me go!" The other people seemed not to notice and he held me in a strangling grip.
>
> *Susan's dream:* I am returning from the mountains. There is ice and snow everywhere. As I approach my house, I see robbers entering. I call the police but they never come. Next I am in jail. My jailer seems to be one of the robbers and I can't understand this. I am in jail because of something to do with my music. I learn that my sister is also in jail and cry bitterly.

When the fertile nature of the feminine is left dry and barren or frozen over with ice and snow, the negative animus claims his victim. He acts autonomously, and in that sense overwhelms the feminine ego with a strangling grip. The woman is helpless. Her ego is not grounded in its feminine nature and thus lacks a vital connection to the strength of the Self. The woman herself cannot differentiate between her ego and the powerful psychic factor which is out to destroy her self-esteem and self-confidence.

Recognizing the negative animus as a separate entity—separate from the ego, the "I"—is a crucial step in a woman's struggle. Susan was able to do this one stormy, sleepless night when she was racked with pain and thoughts of suicide. She said, "*Something* in me wants to kill me." Such a statement was quite unlike her earlier ones: "*I* want to kill myself," or "*I* have no reason to live." She named him The Torturer. Similarly, Mary envisioned her captor as a fiendish dwarf whom she called The Soresucker (aptly, for he kept the psychic wound from healing). Jane's negative animus came as a group of men, who because of their bigger-than-life, destructive character were named The Giants.[10]

Naming the destructive inner voice begins the differentiating process by which the negative animus is depotentiated and the feminine ego is released from tyranny. This motif is reflected in the Grimm fairy tale, "Rumpelstiltskin," where the queen, upon revealing the dwarf's name, is released from her indebtedness to him and the dwarf explodes in rage.

Freed from the ruling edicts of the negative animus, the feminine ego becomes more substantial. The woman no longer feels like a neutered person but begins to take pleasure in her feminine being. She can once again hear, as in Susan's dream, her "music," the harmonic blending and rhythm of her feminine nature. "Music admits us to the depths," writes Emma Jung, "where spirit and nature are still one—or have become one again."[11]

Dreams regularly support the developing feminine ego, as shown in these examples:

Jane's dream: We are somewhere and Nancy gives me a kiss. I worried about who may be there to see but I felt very good. Next we are looking out across a valley to a mountain that contained the Marabar caves [described in E. M. Forster's *Passage to India*]. Nancy said we would go in all the caves.

Mary's dream: B. and I seem to be drawn very close together. We are seated on the floor—crouched down—our right shoulders touching. B. turns toward me and whispers, "This is what the black woman did

---

[10] Jung points out that the animus is often personified as a "collection of condemnatory judges, a sort of College of Preceptors . . . . rather like an assembly of fathers or dignitaries of some kind who lay down incontestable, 'rational,' *ex cathedra* judgments." (*Two Essays in Analytical Psychology,* CW 7, par. 332)

[11] *Animus and Anima,* p. 36.

to me." And in a very secret, private way she kissed me on the lips. It was a wonderful, deep kiss. And she did it again. I enjoyed it so very much.

Susan's dream: I was given a prostitute for my birthday. She was a beautiful woman, graceful and charming. At one point we made love.

The attributes of these female dream companions parallel those of the sacred prostitute. In ancient times she instructed barren women in the art of love-making. The archetypal image of the sacred prostitute comes to these dreamers in similar fashion.

Dreams where a woman (usually an older, revered or beautiful woman, or in some cases the analyst) expresses love or makes love with a woman dreamer are quite common. In fact, such a dream seems necessary at some point in women's lives, and not only for those who have suffered a psychological trauma. It may be considered an initiation rite, for it usually foreshadows positive change, a precursor to the condition in which a woman is no longer split off from her mature sexuality.

In Mary's associations to her dream, B. was described as a "very feminine" acquaintance, a public figure whose capacity for relatedness was well known. Mary felt ill at ease in B.'s presence and harbored negative feelings toward her. Such feelings were clearly irrational, an indication that Mary projected her own split-off feminine nature onto B. In the dream this image of the mature feminine initiates intimate contact. At this time in her development Mary can embrace it, which means she is ready to integrate this side of herself into consciousness.

Many women are somewhat apprehensive when they dream of making love to a woman, fearing that it indicates lesbianism, but this is rarely the case. Even in outer life, passing or temporary lesbian relationships, or erotic desire for another woman, are often expressions of the search for a loving relationship to the feminine. Such a dream usually indicates a shift on the unconscious level, which brings about a corresponding conscious valuing of feminine nature.[12] It can be seen as a beautiful gift from the unconscious, for it makes the dreamer aware of the goddess of love.

---

[12] For a so-called constitutional lesbian or homosexual, dreams of sexual relations with the same sex could not be considered initiatory, as it is in those presented here. (Jung uses the term "constitutional homosexual" in

A woman's developing feminine nature is often imaged in dreams as a girl-child, young and fragile, whom the dreamer must nurture or protect, as in the following examples.

> *Jane's dream:* I am riding horseback across a wooded mountain pass. On the next mountain there is an Indian ceremony in progress. The Indians see me and pursue me shooting arrows, but the arrows fall in bits of brightly colored cloth. Then there is a dark-skinned little girl who runs away from me. At last, after much cajoling, she lets me gently put her hand in mine for a moment.

> *Mary's dream:* I am overlooking this lovely strange valley where a river snakes back and forth through open grassy meadows and dense, wooded forest. I see a young girl. She is the daughter of a pioneer. She is all alone and has been wandering over the land. Now she seems unconscious—I do not think she is sleeping, I think she is unconscious. She is lying on a carpet of green grass on the river bank. Her long brown hair flows out over the ground. She's a lovely little girl. Then some distance away, I see a group of Indians coming. They either have seen her or are looking for her. I want so much to wake her up, to make her conscious again before they find her.

> *Susan's dream:* A little girl comes to me and I agree to care for her. She is eight or nine years old and very difficult but I know I can say the right things to take the poison from her.

In two of these dreams the little girl is found deep within natural settings; she is still contained in the unconscious, prey to primitive psychic forces. Each woman understands the task at hand—to befriend the girl and win her trust, awakening the young feminine to consciousness and healing her wounds. In effect, the dreamer becomes a positive mother to her own burgeoning feminine nature, her psychological maiden.

At a later stage of a woman's psychological development, the positive animus, the stranger, appears. He is the unknown emissary of the gods, the initiator into sexual mysteries combining the physical and spiritual, as in this dream of Jane's:

> A rather bronze-skinned, broad-shouldered man is walking away from me across a small bridge. He doesn't have any clothes on. He turns around and comes toward me. I think to myself that I've never seen a naked man. I am embarrassed and look away.

"The Psychological Aspects of the Kore," *The Archetypes and the Collective Unconscious,* CW 9i, par. 356.)

Then I am one of two women in bed with a man. She is very warm, voluptuous and natural. I make love to the man. It's very pleasant.

The dreamer now observes for the first time the mysterious phallus, the potent masculine component of her own psyche. The stranger animus turns to the dreamer so she may see him clearly. The second part of the dream shows her dynamic feminine side, full-breasted, warm and natural, resembling the image of the sacred prostitute who takes pleasure in relating to a man. In her presence, the dream-ego enjoys making love.

When Jane could accept herself as a woman, other psychic changes came about. The dark, chthonic forces which in her earlier dream were experienced as negative and frightening become positive guides:

Two black men are taking me to see the ocean. It is a special secret place where blacks and slaves have gone for centuries. At first there is a muddy path along a steep ravine, then the path winds around under huge old oak trees. The guide in front begins crawling though narrow openings in large rocks and over and between enormous tree roots. Mostly we are crawling and climbing through things and down things. The ground gets wet and marshy so I know we're getting closer to the ocean.

The narrow path is steep but the dreamer's inner guides are expert in showing the way to the ocean, the deep unconscious, where all life begins. With a new sense of courage stemming from a stronger feminine ego, Jane can now follow them to the archetypal world, a "special secret place" where "blacks and slaves"—instinctive energies and repressed material—have existed for ages. The "wet and marshy" ground suggests that these lost energies belong, in part, to Jane's sexuality. The craggy rocks and dense forest allow for only small rays of light (consciousness) to penetrate this area. The trials and hardships of such a journey are symbolic of the individuation process.

In Mary's case, the dream-meeting with the stranger animus happened quite differently:

I was in the bathroom when a young man came in. I don't know if he was clothed or not, but I took off all my clothes and stood in front of him naked. He seemed uneasy, he may have been embarrassed. I know I was older than he was. He wanted to look at me though, and maybe touch me. I was there for him.

Here the bathroom, instead of being a place to confront and clean up one's personal shit, as in the dreams related earlier, is a place of cleansing and purification. Now the dreamer is ready to accept the Other. He is young because he is an aspect of her masculine side new to her. His youth can also pertain to the young creative *puer* whose spirit enlivens. Although he appears reticent, the dreamer encourages him by enacting the role of the sacred prostitute ("She is getting herself naked and clear of her fear").[13] Her developing feminine ego can allow her body, her loveliness, to be seen and touched by the masculine. This she does openly and without shame.

This dream image made Mary more aware of her feminine nature and more able to accept her sexuality, thereby establishing a better relationship to the goddess of love. In a subsequent dream, maintaining this relationship was depicted as a balancing act performed by cats:

> I was watching several cats as they were lined up sitting on chairs. They were balancing a little shaker of salt on their noses and then passing it on to the next to balance. It was much fun and I felt a sense of delight as I watched their marvelous trick.

Recall the injured or contaminated cat in Mary's earlier dream. Here the cats are quite healthy and playful, in keeping with the gaiety associated with the Egyptian cat goddess Bastet.

Salt is related to Eros. Jung combed alchemical texts to amplify its meaning, concluding that "the most outstanding properties of salt are bitterness and wisdom":

> The factor common to both . . . is, psychologically, the function of *feeling*. Tears, sorrow, and disappointment are bitter, but wisdom is the comforter in all psychic suffering. Indeed, bitterness and wisdom form a pair of alternatives: where there is bitterness wisdom is lacking, and where wisdom is there can be no bitterness. Salt, as the carrier of this fateful alternative, is co-ordinated with the nature of woman.[14]

Elsewhere Jung points out that "salt, in ecclesiastical as well as alchemical usage, is the symbol for Sapientia and also for the distin-

---

[13] See above, p. 23.
[14] *Mysterium Coniunctionis,* CW 14, par. 330.

guished or elect *personality*, as in Matthew 5:13: 'Ye are the salt of the earth.'"[15]

In addition, salt is associated with Venus, whose sign is a circle with a cross below it (the same sign used today to designate female gender). The sign for salt, as used by the early alchemists, is the sign of Venus duplicated four times to form a cross.[16]

Sign for Venus   Sign for salt

The cats' balancing act is an excellent image for what is required in relating to the goddess. If one becomes too one-sided, either by denying sexuality or by making sexuality serve ego desires, then the balance is lost. In recognizing this, the dreamer did indeed experience a sense of delight and joy.

For Susan, conscious development proceeded by keeping alive the two earlier dream images: the beautiful prostitute, given to her for her birthday, who taught her to experience love; and her fragile little girl, representing her own budding feminine nature, who needed to be protected from being poisoned by that old sense of worthlessness which had made her easy prey for men. The psychic changes in Susan were depicted in a dream some months later:

> There is an open church on a hill in a wooded grove. I am in back of the church and see the priest. I become emotional and sexually excited. Next I am in his office seated on a very large red leather couch. The gardener comes in and I see he is the same man as the priest (or his twin). I wish to make love to him but am confused if he is the gardener or the priest.

The open church is reminiscent of the ancient temples of the love goddess, which typically were remote places enclosed by nature.[17] In the time of the sacred prostitute, often it was the priest of the temple who initiated her into the sexual and spiritual rites dedicated to the

---

[15] "A Study in the Process of Individuation," *The Archetypes and the Collective Unconscious,* CW 9i, par. 575.

[16] Ibid.

[17] See Paul Friedrich, *The Meaning of Aphrodite,* p. 74. The ruins of the famous temples to Aphrodite are found in isolated places on Mount Eryx in Sicily and Mount Ida in Greece.

goddess and taught her the art of love-making. The dreamer, sexually aroused, seems ready and willing to be initiated into these mysteries. The stranger animus appears here as both priest, mediator of the divine, and gardener, one familiar with the requirements of nature. Similarly, in the Christian myth, when Mary Magdalene came to the empty tomb she saw the risen Christ but mistook him for the gardener.

The dream is saying that spirituality and nature are one, suggesting that these supposed opposites are becoming more aligned in Susan's psyche. "Nature is not matter only," writes Jung, "she is also spirit. Were that not so, the only source of spirit would be human reason."[18] With such an understanding, women can reach a level of consciousness whereby their feminine being contains forces both instinctively natural and spiritual, blended into a rich elixir of life.

The experience of these three women illustrates a process in which the split-off or degraded aspects of one's feminine nature may be consciously redeemed.

A woman begins by realizing that inappropriate or repressed attitudes and roles are wounding her. She then begins to experience the importance and beauty of her body and sexuality. This supports the connection of the ego to the Self. Attitudes debasing the feminine must be confronted. This is a process of differentiating what actually belongs to "me" from what some evil thing inside is trying to make me believe about myself. Then a sense of the goddess and her devotee, the sacred prostitute, can emerge, allowing and encouraging the woman to love.

As she becomes solicitous toward her undeveloped feminine nature, a woman's ego becomes stronger. The masculine Other, the stranger animus, can be welcomed. He initiates the woman into her essential, independent femininity, a position of strength from which she may relate to both her outer and inner worlds. Fear of men, or guilt at "using" them, ceases to be a problem.

Such a woman simply revels in the experience of love, both the giving and receiving of it.

---

[18] "Paracelsus as a Spiritual Phenomenon," *Alchemical Studies,* CW 13, par. 229.

Ann: A Married Woman

Many women find fulfillment in marriage and become conscious of their feminine nature through the varied circumstances involved in family life. There are many others, however, who do not.

The woman who identifies with the persona role of wife or mother, or becomes psychologically dependent on her husband, never comes to know the full dynamic possibilities of the feminine. With the mother-wife aspect of the feminine so dominant, her own psychological virginity cannot be realized. She may have all the material comforts, yet there is a crying need unheeded. The woman described earlier as having a "chain of tears" around her heart experienced it as a muffled sound and tears on her face, often during intercourse.

It is easy to blame the partner for such dis-ease, but leaving the relationship is not necessarily the answer. Before taking such a drastic step, a woman would be wise to do what she can to establish a good relationship to the goddess. Giving the active side—erotic and joyful—equal expression along with the stable and conservative mother-wife side, can dramatically effect the quality of married life.

Ann was in her mid-forties, married and mother of two teen-age children. She also had a fulfilling professional life Yet she was depressed and experienced a disconcerting emptiness. Returning to school and an interest in social causes offered only temporary relief. She was on the point of leaving her second marriage when she entered analysis. She was searching relentlessly for a man's love, not mother's love or the type of love she shared with her professional colleagues.

For the most part Ann's psychological history appeared healthy. Yet several circumstances had inhibited the development of the dynamic aspect of her feminine nature. She was an adopted child and in her adult years wondered a lot about her biological parents and why they had given her up. Even though her adoptive parents had provided love and security, there remained a deep-seated sense of rejection. (This trauma can also occur in children who are not adopted.)

Her adoptive father died in her early teens. She recalled him as warm and loving, active, with a spirit for fun-making. After his death she became the compliant daughter so as not to create more stress for her mother. In college her second sexual experience resulted in pregnancy and she secretly had an abortion, all alone. Her shame and guilt were buried under a compulsion to do nothing but study. She did not date until she met her husband-to-be almost a year after the abortion.

At the age of thirty-three Ann underwent a mastectomy because of cancer, the same disease her adoptive mother had died from a few years previously. Some years later she also had a hysterectomy, for medical reasons unrelated to the breast surgery. Her diseased feminine organs symbolically pointed to the dis-ease which permeated her psychological life.

On first meeting Ann, I saw a charming woman with a ready smile, apparently quite capable. However, it soon became apparent that this was merely a well-developed persona. She guarded her deeper feelings so well that she could not even reach them herself. Her early traumas continued to be open wounds, although they were now walled off. The sense of abandonment stemming from her adoption, her father's death and her abortion had all contributed to her creation of the wall. That wall had been useful at one time, for as a girl and young woman she had had to prevent the psychological pain from consuming her growing ego; she had built a strong defense and developed useful coping skills.

A dream early in analysis revealed Ann's psychological situation:

> A long black snake has gotten out of its cage and is loose. It goes into a cave. There is a cat in the cave and the cat is afraid of the snake but can't get out of the cave because the snake is in the way. The cat hisses at the snake.

The snake carries a multitude of symbolic meanings, and here it may be interpreted in several ways. It may be seen as the disembodied phallus of the man who had impregnated the undeveloped feminine, represented by the cat. Ann's feminine nature at the time of her first pregnancy was indeed psychologically immature, and the trauma of her abortion, which she underwent on the physical level yet psychologically repressed, fixated her true feminine nature in the womb, the cave.

Or the snake may be viewed as the masculine power of the father. The positive father for the daughter, especially in teen-age years, assists her in becoming aware of the dynamic feminine nature. He supports and strengthens that aspect, enabling the woman to take it into the world of relationships. The mother is a model for the various aspects of the feminine, while the father's influence is instrumental in making them more conscious. Ann's father had communicated to her

Snake goddess.—Faience, from Knossos, Crete.
(Middle Minoan III period; British Museum)

that she was a beautiful and delightful person, and her budding feminine nature grew in awareness of this fact. But his death had
thwarted this development and, as often happens in such situations,
he himself had become a superman in her memory; in Esther Harding's phrase, he became a "ghostly lover," and no actual man could
loosen this psychological bond.[19]

The snake is also associated with the Great Mother, as in the statue
shown on the previous page of a strong, bare-breasted woman with
sturdy arms outstretched, grasping a snake in each hand. From this
point of view the dream shows the maternal aspect of the feminine—
conservative, stable and secure—retaining the dynamic feminine in
the womb-cave. Indeed, appeasing the maternal, being a good
daughter, with all this implies in terms of restricted sexual expression, was the mode of life to which Ann had adapted in her teen-age
years. Thereafter, as an adult, Ann remained the obedient little girl
and like a maiden-princess waited to be rescued by a hero. Marriage
was only another adaptive role, one which continued to repress her
dynamic feminine side.

Overall, the dream pictures a psychological situation where the
dynamic feminine, associated with sexuality and love, is captive in
the unconscious. Ann's deep desire for a mature love relationship
could not find fulfillment because her feminine nature had never been
fully developed or comprehended. More positively, the dream also
showed the possibility of change. The snake is out of its cage (her
defenses have loosened); the cat, symbol of the feminine, is cornered
but ready to fight. Now the dreamer has an opportunity to become
conscious of emotions she has repressed throughout her life.

During her analysis Ann too had bathroom dreams where she had
to clean up the mess; in other dreams she tended to injured young
animals and children. After a good deal of work on herself she
dreamed of a beautiful young woman, image of her inner sacred
prostitute:

> I am lying on the grass with a young woman in her twenties. She
> has long dark hair, loose flowing clothes, a lovely natural face (no
> make-up). We are lying close together, kissing. Warm erotic feelings
> come—also a feeling of being very comfortable with her and liking
> her a lot.

---

[19] *The Way of All Women,* pp. 36f.

Some months later, in active imagination,[20] Ann met the stranger animus:

> I am sitting in a clearing in a forest near a small pool which feeds into a rushing stream. At the edge of the forest is a small wooden chapel. The door is open. (In an earlier active imagination, I tried to approach the chapel and go in, but was prevented from entering by an invisible barrier which surrounded the chapel.) I am sitting on a fallen log looking at the chapel, trying to decide what to do next. Then a man leading a horse walks out of the forest. He has been on a long journey and looks tired and sad. I feel that I know him from somewhere but can't remember where. He is about my age with curly reddish-brown-grey hair and beard, and blue eyes. He sits on the log and begins to speak.
>
> *He:* I have finally caught up with you. I have been trying to get your attention for a long time.
>
> *Me:* Who are you? Have we met before?
>
> *He:* Many times. I am the one you are seeking, the true love. You have seen me in many men and confused them with me. You were seeking in the wrong places. . . . I come to bring you fullness of life.
>
> *Me:* Then why do I want to run away from you and to resist you?
>
> *He:* When you fail to see me, you don't have to struggle with your own creativity and your own power.
>
> *Me:* I don't believe that I am creative or powerful. But tell me, why can't I enter the chapel?
>
> *He:* It is under a spell. . . . No one has been able to enter it for years and years. A priestess is trapped inside and cannot get out.
>
> *Me:* Is there anything we can do?
>
> *He:* That is why we are here. But first you must go fishing. Then we will eat the fish to refresh ourselves.

The dynamic feminine imaged in Ann's early dream as a cat caught in the maternal womb-cave now appears as a priestess trapped in a chapel. This development of the image, from animal to human, is a

---

[20] Active imagination is a method for consciously interacting with unconscious contents. See Jung, "The Transcendent Function," *The Structure and Dynamics of the Psyche,* CW 8, pp. 67-68 and pars. 131ff.

considerable achievement. Although the priestess is still not accessible to conscious understanding, the stranger animus comes out of the forest (the unconscious) to make known her presence and her plight. He is to instruct Ann in the catching and eating of a fish.

The fish, like the snake, is an ancient symbol with many meanings. In Rabbinical literature, it is the symbol of the Messiah who will catch Leviathan and feed him to the Blessed in Paradise. It is the symbol of the Savior in Christian tradition. The fish also belongs to the goddess Astarte, who gave birth to Ichthys (the Greek word for fish), and to Ishtar whose house had the sign of the fish on it, indicating fertility. Psychologically, writes Jung, "the fish signifies an autonomous content of the unconscious." More specifically, it "occasionally signifies the unborn child, because the child before its birth lives in the water like a fish . . . . The fish is therefore a symbol of renewal and rebirth."[21]

Ann's task, then, is to incorporate the meaning of this powerful archetypal image, integrate it into consciousness. This is necessary in order to break the spell on the chapel and free the priestess—the sacred prostitute—symbol of her dynamic feminine side.

The Stranger at the Gate

In the above examples of women on their journeys of individuation, the process has been related to internal psychic events. But it does not take place only there. One truly comes to discern the instinctive feminine nature, the sacred prostitute incarnate in the feminine body, through intimate connection with others. As Esther Harding writes, "The spirituality of the woman must be distilled from concrete experience; it cannot be obtained directly."[22] The internal stranger animus may facilitate the woman's awareness of her sexuality, but it takes an actual man to concretize the experience of love.

An example of this is found in D. H. Lawrence's story, *The Virgin and the Gipsy*. It tells of a young woman, Yvette, who lived in an old rectory with her father, a blind, obese, demanding grandmother, a bitter, aged aunt and her sister. Yvette's life centered around pretty clothes, parties, young men and the anticipation of marriage. One

---

21 *Symbols of Transformation,* CW 5, par. 290 and note 47.
22 *Woman's Mysteries: Ancient and Modern,* p. 150.

day, as if by chance, she met a gipsy. Lawrence describes the effect this stranger has on her previously well-ordered emotions:

> A dandy, in his polished black boots, tight black trousers and tight dark-green jersey, he walked slowly across [the compound]. . . . He looked at Yvette as he passed, staring her full in the eyes, with his pariah's bold yet dishonest stare. Something hard inside her met his stare. But the surface of her body seemed to turn to water. . . .
>
> And as he loped slowly past her, on his flexible hips, it seemed to her still that he was stronger than she was. Of all the men she had ever seen, this one was the only one who was stronger than she was, in her own kind of strength, her own kind of understanding.[23]

> She was truly simple in what she said. It was just what she thought. But it gave no hint of the very different *feeling* that also preoccupied her: the feeling that she had been looked upon, not from the outside, but from the inside, from her secret female self. She was dressing herself up and looking her most dazzling, just to counteract the effect that the gipsy had had on her, when he had looked at her, and seen none of her pretty face and her pretty ways, but just the dark, tremulous, potent secret of her virginity.[24]

> Then she saw the gipsy's face; the straight nose, the slender mobile lips, and the level, significant stare of the black eyes, which seemed to shoot her in some vital, undiscovered place, unerring.[25]

The stranger's eyes penetrate the woman's inner being; his very presence awakens the dormant sacred prostitute and the sensuous feminine nature contained therein. She may hide behind conventional standards, denying her rightful, innate relationship to the goddess of love, but such a screen only delays or aborts her psychic development. Erich Neumann writes, "The moon turns towards the ego and reveals itself or turns away in darkness and disappears."[26] The stranger comes as an emissary of the divine, the moon goddess; if he is not welcomed, the goddess too is slighted and turns her dark side toward the woman. The consequence is that the woman remains cut off from her spirituality, which would contain and enhance her sexual nature.

---

[23] *The Virgin and the Gipsy,* pp. 29f.

[24] Ibid., p. 49.

[25] Ibid., p. 53.

[26] "On the Moon and Matriarchal Consciousness," *Dynamic Aspects of the Psyche,* p. 54.

Often the human man who appears is literally a stranger. There is no romance or overt intention on his part to save the woman from an empty existence. And there are no promises of an enduring relationship. Such a meeting cannot be planned, for that would be plotting, trying to manipulate fate.[27] The woman waits, actively receptive, until one day the man is simply there and she is honestly surprised.

Such an experience occurred in Lisa's life. She was a woman in her early forties, well educated and with a productive career. She had had many romances, had once been married for several years and was currently living with a man in a rather unsettled relationship. She had the attention of many men as she was spirited, entertaining and also compassionate. She instinctively knew how to relate to men, which was her asset but also her curse. She was the typical "anima woman" who unconsciously intuits and becomes the ideal image of the man, but to her own detriment.[28]

Lisa was deeply dissatisfied, for in her relationships she felt that her innermost being was never seen, never loved. For all her independence, her worldliness, her capabilities, she was still waiting for her hero to come, not to take care of her but to love her.

One evening after an eventful day of work in another city, she treated herself to a special dinner at an expensive restaurant. There she met "the stranger," a man from a foreign country who would be returning to it the following day. In their brief time together Lisa was able to experience the sacred prostitute, the dynamic aspect of herself that honored the goddess of love. The resonant beauty of this inner woman was greatly valued and well received by the stranger.

Lisa wrote of her experience as follows:

> I was somewhat alarmed at what was happening to me. I was not out of control, but my control was not as I've always known it, as if something else was intervening. There was some fear and I told him of it. . . . He spoke of the existential fear as if he knew my innermost thoughts. I recall the release I felt in love-making. Release is the only way to explain it. It was a wondrous release! In my shower

---

[27] See Marie-Louise von Franz, *A Psychological Interpretation of the Golden Ass of Apuleius,* p. VII, 5. In a lecture von Franz quotes Jung as saying, "Only one terrible thing can happen to a woman, namely that her power plot might win out. If it is frustrated it is all right but if she gets what she wants then she is lost."

[28] See Harding, *The Way of All Women,* chapter 1, "All Things to All Men."

the next morning, I felt joy, I hugged my body, my beautiful body. I was laughing and singing with a new-found sense of energy and exhilaration. There was no sense of shame or guilt as I often thought there might be, but rather an anticipation of returning home to the man I share my life with.

The release Lisa felt was due to the loosening of the unconscious bond to a certain aspect of maidenhood, much the same as the experience of the initiate in the temple of love. She was released from guilt and inappropriate dependency, released from the compulsion to perform in a certain manner so as to gain or keep a man's attention. Lisa's real being came alive when her sacred prostitute was constellated by the stranger. She allowed her body to respond naturally to the call of love, instead of retreating into her head for an appropriate or clever response. She honored the spiritual essence of the Self. In so doing, she came to know the beauty of her body and her sexuality in an authentic connection to the goddess. The spirit came to life in the body, and Lisa's inner woman became a full participant in her life.

*

The woman who accepts her physical and psychological femininity lives in harmony with the sacred prostitute within. She serves the goddess of love by attending the holy fire of her inner feeling. This is the central warmth of her being, and care must be taken that it does not blaze up to consume, or flicker out. Only in freely chosen service to the goddess is she released from the yoke of servitude to many masters. This enables her to sacrifice ego demands—the need to dominate, to possess, to find security in a man's devotion. The ego then acknowledges a higher authority, the Self.

Women who are conscious of their true feminine being are attentive to the wisdom of the heart; they do not allow this to be contaminated by collective norms and ideals. This wisdom (in men as well as in women) resides in the body and is related to the principle of Eros. Through it women come to realize their true instinctive nature as it unites with the spirit, the male stranger, in the ritual of the sacred marriage.

Birth of the Goddess.—Marble relief, Rome, ca. 500 B.C.
(Museo Nazionale delle Terme, Rome)

5

Restoration of the Soul

> For Wisdom is a loving spirit.
> —Wisdom of Solomon.

> Where Wisdom reigns there is no conflict be-
> tween thinking and feeling.
> —C. G. Jung, *Mysterium Coniunctionis.*

The Split Feminine

The sacred prostitute embodied the spiritual and erotic attributes of
the divine feminine: love and joy, sensuous delight, and also the pain
and suffering associated with love.

But what relevance does her image have today? Is there a place in
our collective conscious value system where she might live again?
And what would that look like?

The sacred prostitute is not merely an abstract concept. As Jung
writes, "concepts are coined and negotiable values. Images are life."[1]
The sacred prostitute's image is one of passion. We know only too
well the look of those without passion for life, their dead anonymous
stare, glimpsed on a busy street or at a cocktail party or, regrettably,
in our own mirrors. The loss of the image parallels the loss of joy
and enthusiasm, leaving us in the throes of a dreadful lethargy. We
endure only by refusing to admit to the emptiness of life, even while
we wish for something to save us.

In Peter Schaffer's highly successful drama, *Equus,* this feeling of
sterility is expressed by the psychiatrist, Dr. Dysart:

> You see, I'm lost . . . . The thing is, I'm desperate. . . . I'm wearing
> that horse's head myself. That's the feeling. All reined up in old lan-
> guage and old assumptions, straining to jump clean-hoofed on to a
> whole new track of being I only suspect is there. I can't see it be-

---

[1] "The Personification of the Opposites," *Mysterium Coniunctionis,* CW
14, par. 226.

cause my educated average head is being held at the wrong angle. I can't jump because the bit forbids it, and my own basic force—my horsepower, if you like—is too little.[2]

Dysart speaks for many individuals unhappy with prevailing Western values—technology as opposed to nature, for instance, or thinking as opposed to feeling. Moreover, the "reins and bits" of patriarchal religious language and cultural assumptions reduce humankind's "basic force" in life by diminishing and debasing the erotic image of the feminine, which in ancient times supported the renewal of life.

The dominant images in the Western world are those of power, wealth and technical knowledge—these are the "gods" we currently honor. We no longer worship the goddess of love; consequently we have no container for sexual ecstasy, the numinous state where the inner core of the individual is awakened and revealed to self and other. Paper hearts and baby cupids hardly suffice; they are symbols of a sentimental romanticism which merely fulfills ego desires. Cupid, the Roman counterpart of the Greek phallic god Eros, has been reduced to a roly-poly, cute cherub with an infantile penis—an image far removed from the potent phallic god who was the consort of the goddess of love.

As the potency ascribed to the phallic god has been reduced or negated, so has the image of the goddess of love fallen into limbo. How can we restore her to life?

Contemporary Western culture, although recently changing, has been based for centuries on white, patriarchal values. Christian mythology, regardless of one's religious preference or heritage, has for two millenniums influenced our attitudes toward the feminine, directly and indirectly. In the patriarchy, the feminine is split off.

> Where the god is male and father only and . . . is associated with law, order, civilization, *logos* and super-ego, religion—and the pattern of life which it encourages—tends to become a matter of these only, to the neglect of nature, instinct, . . . feeling, *eros*, and what Freud called the "id." Such a religion, so far from "binding together" and integrating, may all too easily become an instrument of repression, and so of individual and social disintegration.[3]

---

[2] Peter Schaffer, *Equus,* p. 22.

[3] Father Victor White, quoted in Joan Engelsman, *The Feminine Dimension of the Divine,* p. 40.

The patriarchal attitude, intertwined in the image of a masculine God, in the neglect of the feminine and of instinct and feeling, is apparent in the hierarchical structure, words and tenets of Christian mythology.[4] It is also apparent in unconscious material, as seen below in a priest's dream—which can also be interpreted as a description of the pathology of the Church.[5]

The priest came into analysis because of anxiety attacks. His heart would beat quite rapidly, and he would experience a shortness of breath. A medical examination revealed no physical problem. He was most aware of the anxiety when celebrating the Holy Eucharist; in fact, when it was time to elevate the Holy Elements, he frequently wondered if he could continue. Here is his dream:

> I am assisting in surgery. The head surgeon is on the other side of the operating table. The operation has to do with a malfunction of the heart. We remove the heart and lift it out of the chest cavity, holding it at arm's length above our heads. The heart is much larger then usual and as we lift it, it fills with blood. Then I notice on the back side of the heart, there is a tear, a small hole where the blood leaks out. I am given the job of suturing the hole. At one point I grow afraid. I look at the chief and he nods that everything is all right. As I am suturing the heart it begins to pulsate.

The heart is the seat of love and wisdom ("So teach us to number our days, that we may apply our hearts unto wisdom").[6] The wounded and malfunctioning heart is symbolic of the impaired feeling function within the Church. Blood, the life force, is leaking away. Raising the heart in the dream is like elevating the Elements of the Eucharist, an act of veneration. Only in the act of lifting up, of reverence, can the wounded heart be recognized and mended.

In order to restore the image of the feminine to health, we must first become aware that existing images are inadequate to contain the fullness of life's passionate force. Two images of the feminine are prominent in Western Christianity: Mary Magdalene and the Virgin Mary. Let us look closely at each, and consider their potential as

---

[4] Only males may hold positions of authority in the Church. Although recently women have been ordained in a few denominations, their role as priests or pastors remains secondary to that of men and the liturgy still refers to "God the Father."

[5] See *Memories, Dreams, and Reflections*, p. 175, where Jung illustrates the individual psyche's ability to reflect the collective *Zeitgeist*.

[6] Psalms 90:12.

containers for the love and wisdom symbolized by the goddess and her sacred prostitute.[7]

Mary Magdalene

Marina Warner, in her study of the Virgin Mary, states:

> Together, the Virgin and the Magdalene form a diptych of Christian patriarchy's idea of woman. There is no place in the conceptual architecture of Christian society for a single woman who is neither a virgin nor a whore.[8]

In this conventional view, motherhood and sexuality are divided. Moreover, Mary Magdalene, the sexual side of the diptych, is presumed to have repented her unchaste ways.

> The Magdalene, like Eve, was brought into existence by the powerful undertow of misogyny in Christianity, which associates women with the dangers and degradation of the flesh. For this reason she became a prominent and beloved saint.[9]

She offered hope to mortals who could not attain the perfect state of the Virgin and who sought to be forgiven for their sins.

Mary Magdalene remained a prominent figure in Christian tradition also for a psychological reason. The archetypal dimension of the erotic feminine nature elects a figure to carry its projection; Mary Magdalene carried this projection. The salient point is that human beings, in their spiritual search, must find an image of the feminine which relates to the erotic aspects of the goddess. But the Christian fathers' repression of sexuality manipulated the image so that Mary Magdalene was then seen as penitent, renouncing her sexuality.

Unlike ancient man, whose love of the erotic was not considered incompatible with spirituality, these Christian leaders negated the very element necessary for the renewal of life—the dynamic, transforming, feminine aspect of the psyche.

The figure of Mary Magdalene remains heavily veiled (and burdened) by conventional Christian beliefs, but if we look behind the

---

[7] The discussion in this chapter deals only with the feminine figures in Christian mythology. This is not to deny the equally important feminine images in other world religions,

[8] *Alone of All Her Sex: The Myth and the Cult of the Virgin Mary,* p. 235.

[9] Ibid., p. 225.

I came upon this link in Jerusalem. I walked the Via Dolorosa through the winding, narrow streets of the Old City to observe the stations of the cross. At the eleventh station, now enclosed in the Church of the Holy Sepulchre, there was a beautiful mosaic above the altar. It showed the Virgin Mother draped all in black, standing above the figure of Christ being nailed to the cross laid on the ground. In a near prone position right beside Christ was the deeply anguished Mary Magdalene.

The mosaic depicted her with golden hair, which I found unusual considering her Hebraic origin. In my imagination, I immediately saw the radiant, golden Aphrodite suffering the death of Adonis, her Lord and Master, or the beautiful Inanna grieving over the death of her shepherd king Dumuzi.

In sources other than Christian Scripture we find quite a different image of the Magdalene and her function. In the *Gnostic Gospels,* for instance, she is seen as an active principal in the discipleship of Christ.[12] The Gnostic *Gospel of Philip* relates "the union of man and woman as a symbol of healing and peace, [and] dwells on the relationship of Christ and the Magdalene, who, it says, was often kissed by him."[13] It describes Mary Magdalene as "Jesus' most intimate companion, and the symbol of Divine Wisdom."[14]

> The companion of [the Savior is] Mary Magdalene. [But Christ loved] her more than [all] the disciples and used to kiss her [often] on her [mouth]. The rest of [the disciples were offended by it. . .]. They said to him, "Why do you love her more than all of us?" The Savior answered and said to them, "Why do I not love you as [I love] her?"[15]

According to the *Dialogue of the Savior,* Mary Magdalene was a disciple. Moreover, she was one of the three disciples to receive special teaching and was praised above Matthew and Thomas, the other two. It was said that "she spoke as a woman who knew the All."[16]

---

[12] See Elaine Pagels, *The Gnostic Gospels,* p. xv. These documents come from codices discovered in Nag Hammadi in 1945.

[13] Warner, *Alone of All Her Sex,* p. 229.

[14] Pagels, *The Gnostic Gospels,* p. 77.

[15] Ibid.

[16] Ibid.

The attention Mary Magdalene received, in addition to her capabilities and her sex, created rivalry between her and the male disciples. In *Pistis Sophia* (Faith Wisdom) there is an account of Peter becoming angry because Mary Magdalene is dominating the conversation with Jesus. Peter is fearful that his position of leadership in the new religious community is diminishing.

> He urges Jesus to silence her and is quickly rebuked. Later, however, Mary admits to Jesus that she hardly dares speak to him freely because, in her words, "Peter makes me hesitate; I am afraid of him because he hates the female race." Jesus replies that whoever the Spirit inspires is divinely ordained to speak, whether man or woman.[17]

On another occasion, as written in *The Gospel of Mary,* Mary Magdalene was asked by the disciples, disheartened and terrified after the crucifixion, to encourage them by speaking of the things Jesus had told her privately. Instead of relating something from the past, she recounts a vision of Christ she has had and what this vision revealed to her. The others doubt and rebuff her:

> Mary wept and said to Peter, "My brother Peter, what do you think? Do you think that I thought this up myself in my heart? Do you think I am lying about the Savior? Levi answered and said to Peter, "Peter, you have always been hot-tempered. . . . If the Savior made her worthy, who are you to reject her!"[18]

This image of Mary Magdalene as a chosen, even favored, disciple contrasts greatly with the orthodox view of her as a penitent whore. In the *Gnostic Gospels* she is a capable, active, loving woman with the ability to know and to speak "the All"—which perhaps refers to the highest Wisdom, a certain understanding the heart receives and contains. Mary Magdalene had the ability to know inexplicable things, as in her vision of Christ. She did not question it, as did the other disciples; she trusted her innermost source. She could see the divine emissary and pass His message on to humans. Like the sacred prostitute, she mediated between the world of the divine and the world of humans.

There are myths which depict Mary Magdalene's ability to perform miracles. One tells of when she saw and spoke to the risen Christ, as

---

[17] Ibid., p. 78.

[18] Ibid., p. 15

it is believed she was the first to do. She hurried off to tell the other disciples. On her way, she met Pontius Pilate and told him of the wondrous news. "Prove it," Pilate said. At that moment a woman carrying a basket of eggs passed by and Mary Magdalene took one in her hand. As she held it up before Pilate, the egg turned a brilliant red.[19] To attest to the legendary event, in the cathedral which bears her name in Jerusalem there stands a beautiful statue of Mary Magdalene holding a colored egg.

The egg is very appropriate in this context since it is symbolic of new life and the capacity for giving birth. The colored egg is also associated with Astarte, goddess of spring, from whose name our word "Easter" is derived.[20] Colored eggs were used in the spring celebrations honoring the goddess, as they are today at Easter.

Another myth, coming from Christian tradition and acclaimed in the sixth station of the cross, tells of a woman who wiped the dust, sweat and blood from Jesus' face as he walked the path to Calvary. The likeness of Jesus' face was imprinted on her clean linen. Through time and tradition the woman has been called Veronica, but this name speaks more to the act than the name. "Veronica" is a combination of "true" (Latin *vera*) and "image" (*icona*). This has led to speculation about whether indeed there was a woman named Veronica, or if this woman might have been Mary Magdalene.

No one can really say for sure. But more important is the psychological significance of the myth, namely that the active feminine nature holds the image of the divine. As the completing element, it is the feminine nature which leads one to the Self.

Another facet of a reconsidered Mary Magdalene comes from composers Tim Rice and Andrew Webber in the rock opera *Jesus Christ Superstar.* Here she is portrayed as a profane prostitute who fell in love with the man Jesus, not the Savior, and by her love was transformed. She is depicted as the one who soothes and calms her lover. The lyrics suggest that she was much like the sacred prostitute ("The ointment's sweet for the fire in your head and feet . . . close your eyes and relax"):[21]

---

[19] This story was told to me by a nun in the Cathedral of Mary Magdalene.

[20] Ernest Klein, *A Comprehensive Etymological Dictionary of the English Language,* p. 235.

[21] "Everything's Alright," lyrics by Tim Rice, music by Andrew Lloyd Webber, copyright 1969 by Leeds Music Corporation.

In the past few days when I've seen myself
I seem like someone else.[22]

Mary Magdalene, then, from a viewpoint not restricted by patriarchal attitudes, is a feminine figure to which women can relate without betraying their essential nature. Her image, like that of the sacred prostitute, is capable of carrying all the dynamic and transforming aspects of the feminine—passion, spirituality and joyfulness.

The Virgin Mary and the Black Madonna

The other half of the Christian diptych portrays the Virgin Mother. She is the idealization of womanhood, a person of absolute purity upon whom falls no sin. She too was human, but more than human, since Christian tradition decrees her bodily assumption into Heaven. Does she, like Mary Magdalene, have archetypal precedents? Is there, behind her traditionally accepted image, a more complete picture of the vibrant fullness and fertility of feminine nature?

When we review the attributes of the goddesses, from the early civilization of Sumer to the highly artistic civilizations of Greece and Rome, we discover that the characteristics they shared were physical beauty, virginity, association with the moon and the tragic death, or deliberate sacrifice, of a son-lover.

With this in mind, consider the image of Mary, mother of Jesus. She is worshiped as the Virgin Mary. Indeed, it is her virginity (the state of being chaste, not the original meaning of the word) which sets her apart from other women. Mary is also associated with the cosmos, often being called Queen of Heaven. To depict her heavenly beauty, she is frequently pictured enthroned on the moon. Her primary association is with her son, who is sacrificed; Mary's role as a wife is negligible.

Despite these parallels with the image of the goddess, Mary is conventionally associated solely with the maternal aspect of the feminine—static and protective. The dynamic, transforming aspect, related to the passion, sexuality and fertility of the love goddesses, is conspicuously lacking.

---

22 Ibid., "I Don't Know How to Love Him."

However, there are other correlations between Mary and the ancient chthonic goddesses which, though not commonly known, are operative in collective consciousness. In a small number of cathedrals throughout Europe, both in popular and isolated places, a black madonna is venerated. She is not the more familiar, angelic madonna in the blue cloak, but one as black as the earth itself. She belongs to the lower world, not the heavenly realm.[23]

From prehistoric times, as early as thirty thousand years before the beginning of the Christian era, comes the Black Venus of Lespugue, carved from a mammoth tusk, now preserved in the Musée de l'Homme in Paris. As she predates a time when any knowledge of agriculture existed, she is more than earth; she is Life itself. Other black feminine images, symbolic of the chthonic life force, have been worshiped throughout the ages.

In Tindari, on the coast of the Mediterranean in eastern Sicily, a black statue of the madonna bears the inscription, *nigra sum sed formosa*—"I am black, but comely"—from the Song of Solomon 1:5. Christian scholars interpret this passage as referring to a bride, the Virgin Mary as Ecclesia, uniting in marriage with the bridegroom, her son Christ. It appears to be founded in the sacred marriage rite of Ishtar and Tammuz, since there are many parallels between the ancient cuneiform tablets and this Old Testament text. Could not this "black and comely" madonna be a product of the far more ancient image of the goddess?

Another image is found in a monastery in the center of Switzerland—the black madonna of Einsiedeln. Her original color was not black, but the flesh color of the Europeans. Through the centuries, however, due to the smoke from the large votive candles which surrounded her, she became black. About two centuries ago an artist restored her to her original color, but the people expressed doubts concerning the genuineness of the renewed image, since many miracles had previously been attributed to her blackness. The artist was then asked to paint her black again. Those who worshiped her "wanted her to be black because she is a religious expression with archetypal grounding."[24]

---

[23] I am indebted to Gilles Quispel for much of the information here on the black madonna, taken from his lecture on the subject at Emory University, November 7, 1984.

[24] Ibid.

The Black Madonna of Einsiedeln, Switzerland.

Perhaps the most celebrated black madonna is called Our Lady Under The Earth, found in the cathedral of Chartres, south of Paris. The actual statue replaces a much older one which according to legend was venerated by the Druid priests long before Christ's birth. In fact, the church today stands on the very foundations of an ancient Gallo-Roman sanctuary.

In the old world, the custom of rebuilding the churches on the original site of the temple to the goddess, or even resanctifying the existing structure, was quite common. In Ephesus and Baalbek, the Christian churches were originally shrines to Aphrodite. Santa Maria Maggiore, in Rome, was built over the sacred cave of the Magna Mater.

In Crete, the main sanctuary in Kritiza is dedicated to Mary as the Pankagia Kjore, The Most Holy Lady. This was the same title given to Ariadne, a princess of Crete, who as we have seen in chapter 2 was associated with Aphrodite.

It was the black madonna of Montserrat who inspired Goethe to write the closing lines of *Faust,* where Mary appears and saves Dr. Faustus. "The eternally feminine elevates us to herself." This phrase speaks to the woman eternal; "it is not the divine element in woman, but the divine as woman."[25] Scholarly commentaries on Goethe's work acknowledge the influence of the Montserrat madonna, yet they fail to mention that she is black.

When women adapted to the religious tenets of the patriarchy, they also accepted man's image of his anima as an accurate reflection of feminine nature. They thereby lost their connection to the genuine feminine, including the chthonic aspects represented by the black madonna.

Many black madonnas are currently valued as religious symbols, but far more numerous are images of the conventional "blue" madonnna. The latter, as anima, inspired men to build impressive cathedrals and create beautiful works of art, but she lacks a crucial dimension of feminine nature.

The black madonna, associated with both the earth and fertility, is an image of the divine feminine reflecting the ancient connection between women's nature and the goddess of love. Through her, the Great Goddess still lives in Christianity.

---

[25] Ibid.

The Goddess through Time

The unconscious regularly bridges the gap between modern-day religious attitudes and the ancient realm of the goddess. Her continuing presence was made known to me in the following dream I had while visiting Jerusalem.

> I was walking the dark, narrow streets of the old city. I saw many tiny cavelike shops carved out in these ancient walls. At one such shop there was a crudely made table in front of a small doorway. On the table was a rabbit whose belly had been opened and numerous baby rabbits were being removed. The babies were slick and shiny, and although fully formed they were still curled in an egg-shaped position. These "eggs" were placed in a pile next to the mother rabbit and covered with a moist cloth to keep them warm. On seeing this sight, with a sense of awe and feeling great emotion, I exclaimed with profound joy, "Now I know the meaning of Easter!"

I had been immersed in the historical religious ambience of this unique city; yet my dream took me to a more remote time, a time when the goddess enabled the renewal of life. The ritual animal of the goddess is the rabbit, associated with fertility. The eggs in the dream symbolize new life. Both eggs and rabbits still have a prominent place in Easter festivities. Easter, from my Christian background, was associated with death and resurrection, but the dream made me aware that it also means new life and the fertility of the feminine nature in connection to the goddess.

There are also correlations between the love goddess and the image of Sophia/Wisdom in Judeo-Christian tradition. The hymns in which the love goddesses and Wisdom describe themselves as the divine feminine being who presides over heaven and earth and all created things are remarkably similar. The creators of the following hymns, although separated by time and distance, portrayed both the majesty and boundless influence of the divine feminine nature.

Inanna's Hymn:

> At the end of the day, the Radiant Star, the Great Light that fills the sky,
> The Lady of the Evening appears in the heavens.
> The people in all the lands lift their eyes to her. . .
> The four-footed creatures of the high steppe,
> The lush gardens and orchards, the green reeds and trees,
> The fish of the deep and the birds in the heavens. . .

The living creatures and the numerous people of Sumer kneel
before her.[26]

The cosmic force of Aphrodite is described by Euripides in *Hippolytus:*

Wide o'er man my realm extends, and proud the name that I, the
goddess Cypris, bear, both in heaven's courts and 'mongst all those
who dwell within the limits of the sea and the bounds of Atlas,
beholding the sun's light.[27]

The invocation to Venus, as recorded by Lucretius, begins:

Mother of Aeneas and his race, delight of men and gods, life-giving
Venus, it is your doing that under the wheeling constellations of the
sky all nature teems with life, both the sea that buoys up our ships
and the earth that yields our food. Through you all living creatures
are conceived and come forth to look upon the sunlight. . . . you
alone are the guiding power of the universe and without you nothing
emerges into the shining sunlit world to grow in joy and loveliness.[28]

The realm, the power and life-giving qualities of the divine feminine are shared also by Sophia/Wisdom. In Ecclesiasticus 24:3-18,
Wisdom says of herself:

I came out of the mouth of the most High,
    and covered the earth as a cloud.
I dwelt in high places,
    and my throne is in a cloudy pillar.
I alone encompassed the circuit of heaven,
    and walked in the bottom of the deep.
I had power over the waves of the sea, and over
    all the earth, and over every people and nation. . . .
I was exalted like a cedar in Libanus,
    and as a cypress tree upon the mountains of Hermon. . . .
I gave a sweet smell like cinnamon and aspalathus,
    and I yielded a pleasant odour like the best myrrh.
As the vine brought I forth pleasant savour,
    and my flowers are the fruit of honour and riches.
I am the mother of fair love,

---

[26] Diane Wolkstein and S.N. Kramer, *Inanna: Queen of Heaven and Earth,* p.
101.

[27] Paul Friedrich, *The Meaning of Aphrodite,* p. 94.

[28] Ibid., p. 217.

and fear, and knowledge and holy hope:
I therefore, being eternal, am given to all my children
which are chosen of him.[29]

Wisdom's majestic domain knows no boundaries, nor did the goddess. As seen in the earlier chapters, she is associated with the sweet-smelling scents, the perfumes of nature used by the goddesses. Amplifying Wisdom's description of herself, Jung writes:

> As Ruach, the spirit of God, she brooded over the waters of the beginning. Like God, she has her throne in heaven. . . .
> She is the feminine numen . . . . a reflection of Ishtar . . . . This is confirmed by the detailed comparison of Wisdom with trees, such as the cedar, palm, terebinth ("turpentine tree"), olive, and cypress, etc. All these trees have from ancient times been symbols of the Semitic love- and mother-goddess. A holy tree always stood beside her altar on high places. . . . Like the Holy Ghost, Wisdom is given as a gift to the elect . . . .
> . . . . She is sent from heaven and from the throne of glory as a "Holy Spirit." As a psychopomp she leads the way to God and assures immortality.[30]

Her co-existence with Yahweh signifies the perpetual *hieros gamos* from which worlds are begotten and born.[31]

No matter what her name, the love goddess is related to the earth, the body, to passion, sexuality and fertility. She is the moving, transforming, mystical power of love which unites the human element with the divine. The feminine images in Christian mythology— Mary Magdalene, the Virgin Mary, Wisdom and the Holy Spirit— can all carry this dynamic meaning when their full nature is reinstated.

The image of the divine goddess who embodies the smiling, radiant, independent and sensuous aspects of feminine nature has existed since recorded history. It can continue to exist in our time if we allow her image to be reestablished and take its rightful place in conscious understanding.

---

[29] Quoted by Jung in "Answer to Job," *Psychology and Religion: West and East,* CW 11, par. 610.

[30] Ibid., pars. 611-613.

[31] Ibid., par. 624.

In Search of Integration

Reinstating the image of the goddess appears to be a herculean task, for the patriarchy does not readily share its power. Yet the past several decades have seen significant changes. The consciousness-raising efforts of the feminist movement have brought to the forefront the need for equality between women and men. Woman's attributes are becoming understood in roles other than wife and mother.

Changes no less significant are taking place in the internal world; the split-off aspect of the divine feminine is being healed from within. The healing consists of integrating the ancient feminine images in such a way that we can relate to them through our own cultural mythology.

An example of this phenomenon comes from the unconscious of a woman who had previously been a devout Catholic. The Church had provided a way of life connected to spirituality, but only up to a certain point. In her adult years she found in Church teachings no sense of enlightenment or support for her sense of herself as woman. In fact, quite the opposite—she felt she was drying up, her spiritual life was diminishing.

After enduring a severe illness and other personal problems, she left the Church to seek other avenues of spiritual development. At one point she had many dreams of the Church and symbols of Christianity being reduced to ruin and ashes. She became more conscious of the wholeness of her feminine nature; she was more than a perfect wife and mother.[32] But not wanting to split off her faith, the question now became one of how to reconcile her new consciousness of feminine nature with images of the feminine in Christian mythology. The transformation process was shown in a dream:

> I had entered an old, beautiful house. In the front room a dozen or so women were sitting in a circle. They were celebrating some religious rite. I wandered to the back of the house. There I found a small chapel. The altar had been readied for Mass but no one was there. Then I rejoined the other women and as I entered I brought into their group a statue of the Virgin Mary.

The circle of women "celebrating some religious rite" is reminiscent of the ancient cults of women who kept alive the mysteries of the

---

[32] Jung notes that "*perfection* is a masculine desideratum, while woman inclines by nature to *completeness*." (Ibid., par. 620; his emphasis)

feminine. In her personal search, the dreamer had come to an appreciation of these mysteries. The Christian ritual of Mass was no longer an active factor in her life; it had been relegated to the back of her psychic "house." But now she brings an image from that place, a statue of Mary, to be consciously integrated into her new-found understanding of feminine nature

Another dream, by a priest, demonstrates the dire plight of the feminine in relation to orthodox teachings of the Church:

> The bishop and I are walking along a road. There is farm and swamp land and we are crossing a bridge. We see a huge white bird—larger than a person—caught in the roots of a tree. The bird is calling to us, saying that she can do great wonders and favors for us. I recognize that she is in distress and cannot help herself. I take one of her wings and untangle it from the tree she has fallen in.
>
> I call the bishop and he kneels and says a prayer; he reaches over into her body, showing himself and me how old her skin and bones are. She is calmed and asks to see the bishop's amulets. He opens a little string purse and shows her three charms carved from bone. One is a cross of bones. Another is an anchor almost in the shape of a heart. The third, I'm not quite sure, maybe a little vial in the shape of a figure eight.

The dream is set in the realm of the Great Mother: fertile soil, swamps and water. There is a crossover to the land of the unconscious. On the objective level, the bishop is a symbol of the organized, hierarchical Church. On the subjective level, the bishop is analogous to the dreamer's own inner spiritual authority, a symbol of the Self. The white bird, symbol of peace, relates to the imagery of both Aphrodite and the Holy Spirit. It is enormous, larger than life, as if to emphasize the gravity of the situation.

When a factor important for psychic health is undervalued or ignored in conscious life, its proportions and significance will be correspondingly magnified in the unconscious. Here we see the unconscious compensating for the conscious lack of reverence for feminine nature. The tree is the ensnaring factor which prevents the white bird from being free.

The tree, another ancient symbol with many meanings, is associated in the dreamer's psychology with the cross, emblem of Christianity. In Christian art the cross is often depicted by a living tree, that which dies each year and is resurrected to new life. In the legendary Tree of Life, the cosmic tree connecting heaven, earth and the underworld, there is often a bird in the top branches, but here the bird has fallen and become caught in the roots. In other words, the image of Aphrodite, or the feminine aspect of the Holy Spirit, is trapped in the roots of Christian tradition—just as, when monotheism originated, the attributes of the goddess of love were ensnared in negative attitudes toward the flesh.

The bishop, representing both the dreamer's inner spiritual authority and the external authority of the Church, has in his possession secret charms, primitive talismans made of bones. They are reminiscent of a shaman's amulets, which are often exquisitely carved to represent the spirit helper. They are worn around the shaman's neck, sewn to his garments or hidden within a bundle. One of the bishop's bone amulets is a vial like a figure eight. In antiquity such vials contained the most precious fluids, perfumes or a healing elixir. The vial is symbolic of the feminine as container.

The anchor is symbolic of Christ;[33] its nearly-heart shape relates it to the feeling function. It is also associated with the Virgin Mary: the shank and stock of the anchor, the body of Christ, rises from the horizontal blade in the form of a crescent, ancient symbol of the goddess of love.

The cross of bones is symbolic of death and resurrection. In Ezekiel's vision, the dry bones rose to life when the Spirit descended and breathed a soul upon them. Bones are also considered the seat of the soul, the fundamental structural framework upon which everything else is placed.

The three amulets thus comprise those magical ingredients essential to the more profound spiritual life the dreamer was seeking, the basic framework into which the feminine spirit can descend to inspire the life of the soul. This ancient knowledge is held subjectively by the inner authority of the dreamer and objectively by the Church. How these distinctive and powerful images are to be used is still another question—one the dream does not answer.

Such images are active in the unconscious of humankind, and in individual ways are being brought to consciousness. A dynamic, transforming feminine image does exist in our Western Christian tradition, but the missing attributes of the goddess can only be restored to the collective by each one of us, in our individual way, enlarging our perception of the feminine.

---

[33] "Which hope we have as an anchor of the soul."—Hebrews 6:19.

Down through the ages, women have been the repository for the meaning, emotions and values attributed to the goddess of love. In valuing the joyful, self-confident and sensuous nature of her priestess, the sacred prostitute, both men and women connect with something of value in themselves. Women can then carry this vital aspect of feminine nature into the world. Men can once again become open to the dynamic aspect of the feminine and thereby facilitate necessary modifications in political, social, economic and religious structures.

In this way, humankind can restore to consciousness the creative and loving force of the feminine nature, that which so long ago was embodied in the sacred prostitute.

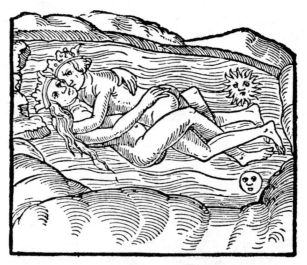

Alchemical image of the sacred marriage, union of opposites (king and queen, sun and moon):

O Luna, folded in my sweet embrace,
Be you as strong as I, as fair of face.
O Sol, brightest of all lights known to men,
And yet you need me, as the cock the hen.
　　—from *Rosarium philosophorum* (1550).

Bibliography

Allen, Donald and Tallman, Warren, eds. *Poetics of the New American Poetry.* New York: Grove Press, 1973.

Ball, John. ed. *From Beowulf to Modern British Writers.* New York: The Odyssey Press, 1959.

Barnstone, Aliki and Barnstone, Willis, eds. *A Book of Women Poets from Antiquity to Now.* New York: Schocken Books, 1980.

Briffault, Robert. *The Mothers: A Study of the Origins of Sentiments and Institutions.* London: George Allen and Unwin, 1927.

Caxton, William. *The Golden Legend or Lives of the Saints,* vol. 4. New York: AMS Press, 1973.

Campbell, Joseph. *The Hero with a Thousand Faces* (Bollingen Series XVII). Princeton: Princeton University Press, 1949.

_____. *Myths to Live By.* New York: Viking Press, 1972.

Chicago, Judy. *The Dinner Party: A Symbol of our Heritage.* Garden City: Anchor Press, 1979.

Claremont de Castillejo, Irene. *Knowing Woman.* New York: G.P. Putnam's Sons, 1973.

Clark, Kenneth. *Feminine Beauty.* New York: Rizzoli International Publications, 1980.

Davies, Robertson. *Fifth Business.* New York: Viking Press, 1970.

De Beauvoir, Simone. *The Second Sex.* New York: Alfred Knopf, 1953.

Downing, Christine. *Mythological Images of the Feminine.* New York: Crossroads, 1984.

Eban, Abba. *Heritage: Civilization of the Jews.* New York: Simon and Schuster, 1984.

Engelsman, Joan. *The Feminine Dimension of the Divine.* Philadelphia: The Westminster Press, 1979.

Ferguson, George. *Signs and Symbols in Christian Art.* New York: Oxford University Press, 1954.

Frazer, James G. *The Golden Bough: A Study in Magic and Religion,* vol. 2. London: MacMillan and Co., 1934.

_____. *The Golden Bough: A Study in Magic and Religion,* vol. 1, part 4. 3rd edition. New York: St. Martin's Press, 1914.

163

Friedrich, Paul. *The Meaning of Aphrodite.* Chicago: The University of Chicago Press, 1978.

Freud, Sigmund. "The Psychology of Women." *New Introductory Lectures on Psychoanalysis,* tr. W. J. H. Sprott. New York: 1933.

_____. "Some Psychical Consequences of the Anatomical Distinction between the Sexes," *The Complete Psychological Works of Sigmund Freud,* vol. 19. London: Hogarth Press, 1953-1966.

Goldberg, B. F. *The Sacred Fire: The Story of Sex in Religion.* New York: Horace Liveright, 1930.

Graves, Robert. *The White Goddess.* New York: Farrar, Straus and Giroux, 1948.

Hall, Nor. *The Moon and the Virgin.* New York: Harper and Row, 1980.

Harding, M. Esther. *The Way of All Women.* New York: G. P. Putnam's Sons, 1970.

_____. *Woman's Mysteries: Ancient and Modern.* New York: Harper Colophon Books, 1971.

Hastings, James, ed. *Encyclopaedia of Religion and Ethics,* vol. 6. Edinburgh: T. and T. Clark, 1956.

Heidel, Alexander. *The Gilgamesh Epic and Old Testament Parallels.* Chicago: Chicago University Press, 1949.

Hesse, Herman. *Steppenwolf.* Tr. Basil Creighton. Middlesex: Penguin, 1965.

The Homeric Hymns. Trans. Charles Boer. Irving, Texas: Spring Publications, 1979.

Hooke, S.H. *Babylonian and Assyrian Religion.* Norman: University of Oklahoma Press, 1963.

The I Ching or Book of Changes. Trans. Richard Wilhelm. Princeton: Princeton University Press, 1950.

Jung, C. G. *The Collected Works* (Bollingen Series XX). 20 vols. Trans. R.F.C. Hull. Ed. H. Read, M. Fordham, G. Adler, Wm. McGuire. Princeton: Princeton University Press, 1953-1979.

_____. *Memories, Dreams and Reflections.* Tr. Richard and Clara Winston. Ed. Aniela Jaffé. New York: Vintage Books, 1963.

Jung, C. G., et. al. *Man and His Symbols.* New York: Doubleday and Company, 1964.

Jung, Emma. *Animus and Anima.* Zurich: Spring Publications, 1974.

Klein, Ernest. *A Comprehensive Etymological Dictionary of the English Language*. Amsterdam: Elsevier Scientific Publishing Company, 1971.

Kramer, Samuel. *The Sacred Marriage Rite*. Bloomington: Indiana University Press, 1969.

Lawrence, D. H. *St. Mawr and The Man Who Died*. New York: Vintage Books, 1953.

⸻. *The Virgin and the Gipsy*. New York: Vintage Books, 1984.

Layard, John. *The Virgin Archetype*. Zurich: Spring Publications, 1972.

Michener, James. *The Source*. New York: Random House, 1965.

The Nag Hammadi Library. Ed. James M. Robinson. San Francisco: Harper and Row, 1981.

Neumann, Erich. "The Psychological Stages of Feminine Development." *Spring 1959*. New York: The Analytical Psychology Club of New York.

⸻. *The Great Mother: An Analysis of the Archetype*. Trans. Ralph Manheim. New York: Pantheon Books, 1955.

⸻. "On the Moon and Matriarchal Consciousness." *Dynamic Aspects of the Psyche*. Trans. H. Nagel. New York: The Analytical Psychology Club, 1956.

New Larousse Encyclopedia of Mythology. London: Hamlyn, 1976.

Otto, Walter. *Dionysus: Myth and Cult*. Dallas: Spring Publications, 1981.

Pagels, Elaine. *The Gnostic Gospels*. New York: Vingage Books, 1981.

Patai, Raphael. *The Hebrew Goddess*. KTAV Publishing House, n.d.

Perera, Sylvia Brinton. *Descent to the Goddess: A Way of Initiation for Women*. Toronto: Inner City Books, 1981.

Quispel, Gilles. *The Black Madonna*. Unpublished manuscript.

Sanger, William W. *History of Prostitution*. New York: Harper and Brother, 1859.

Schaffer, Peter. *Equus*. New York: Avon Books, 1974.

Seaford, Richard. *Pompeii*. Summerfield Press, 1978. (Distributed by Thames and Hudson, New York.)

The Simon and Schuster Book of the Opera. New York: Simon and Schuster, 1977.

Stein, Robert. "The Animus and Impersonal Sexuality." *Spring 1970*. New York: The Analytical Psychology Club of New York.

Stone, Merlin. *When God Was a Woman.* New York: Harcourt, Brace, Jo-vanovich, 1976.

Stassinopoulos, Arianna and Beny, Roloff. *The Gods of Greece.* New York: Harry N. Abrams, 1983.

Thompson, Clara. *Psychoanalysis: Evolution and Development.* New York: Hermitage House, 1950.

Thompson, William. *The Time Falling Bodies Take to Light.* New York: St. Martin's Press, 1981.

Ulanov, Ann. *The Feminine in Jungian Psychology and in Christian Theology.* Evanston: Northwestern University Press, 1971.

Von Franz, Marie-Louise. *Alchemy: Introduction to the Symbolism and the Psychology.* Toronto: Inner City Books, 1980.

_____. *On Divination and Synchronicity: The Psychology of Meaningful Chance.* Toronto: Inner City Books, 1980.

_____. *Problems of the Feminine in Fairy Tales.* Zurich: Spring Publications, 1972.

_____. *A Psychological Interpretation of the Golden Ass of Apuleius.* New York: Spring Publications, 1970.

_____. *Puer Aeternus: A Psychological Study of the Adult Struggle with the Paradise of Childhood.* 2nd ed. Santa Monica: Sigo Press, 1981.

_____. *Shadow and Evil in Fairytales.* Zurich: Spring Publications, 1974.

Walker, Barbara. *The Woman's Encyclopedia of Myths and Secrets.* San Francisco: Harper and Row, 1983.

Wall, O. A. *Sex and Sex Worship.* St. Louis: C. V. Mosby Company, 1919.

Warner, Marina. *Alone of All Her Sex: The Myth and the Cult of the Virgin Mary.* New York: Alfred A. Knopf, 1976.

Wolkstein, Diane and Kramer, S. N. *Inanna: Queen of Heaven and Earth.* New York: Harper and Row, 1983.

Woodman, Marion. *Addiction to Perfection: The Still Unravished Bride.* Toronto: Inner City Books, 1982.

_____. *The Pregnant Virgin: A Process of Psychological Transformation.* Toronto: Inner City Books, 1985.

Index

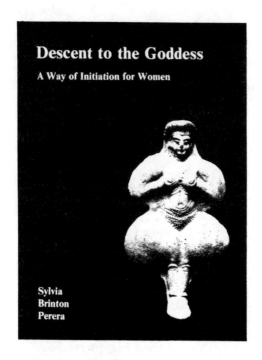

Descent to the Goddess

A Way of Initiation for Women

Sylvia
Brinton
Perera

6. Descent to the Goddess: A Way of Initiation for Women.
Sylvia Brinton Perera (New York). ISBN 0-919123-05-8. 112 pp.

A highly original and provocative book about women's freedom and the need for an inner, female authority in a masculine-oriented society.

Combining ancient texts and modern dreams, the author, a practising Jungian analyst, presents a way of feminine initiation. Inanna-Ishtar, Sumerian Goddess of Heaven and Earth, journeys into the underworld to Ereshkigal, her dark "sister," and returns. So modern women must descend from their old role-determined behavior into the depths of their instinct and image patterns, to find anew the Great Goddess and restore her values to modern culture.

Men too will be interested in this book, both for its revelations of women's essential nature and for its implications in terms of their own inner journey.

"The most significant contribution to an understanding of feminine psychology since Esther Harding's *The Way of All Women.*"—**Marion Woodman,** Jungian analyst and author of *Addiction to Perfection, The Pregnant Virgin* and *The Owl Was a Baker's Daughter.*

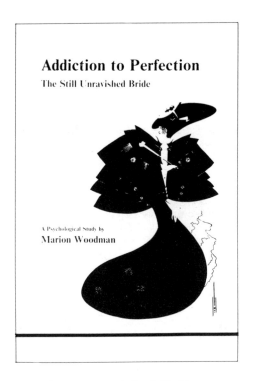

Addiction to Perfection
The Still Unravished Bride

A Psychological Study by
Marion Woodman

12. Addiction to Perfection: The Still Unravished Bride.
Marion Woodman (Toronto). ISBN 0-919123-11-2. 208 pp.

"This book is about taking the head off an evil witch." With these words Marion Woodman begins her spiral journey, a powerful and authoritative look at the psychology and attitudes of modern woman.

The witch is a Medusa or a Lady Macbeth, an archetypal pattern functioning autonomously in women, petrifying their spirit and inhibiting their development as free and creatively receptive individuals. Much of this, according to the author, is due to a cultural one-sidedness that favors patriarchal values—productivity, goal orientation, intellectual excellence, spiritual perfection, etc.—at the expense of more earthy, interpersonal values that have traditionally been recognized as the heart of the feminine.

Marion Woodman's first book, *The Owl Was a Baker's Daughter: Obesity, Anorexia Nervosa and the Repressed Feminine,* focused on the psychology of eating disorders and weight disturbances.

Here, with a broader perspective on the same general themes, she continues her remarkable exploration of women's mysteries through case material, dreams, literature and mythology, in food rituals, rape symbolism, Christianity, imagery in the body, sexuality, creativity and relationships.

"It is like finding the loose end in a knotted mass of thread. . . . What a relief! Somebody knows!"—**Elizabeth Strahan**, *Psychological Perspectives.*

Studies in Jungian Psychology
by Jungian Analysts

Sewn Paperbacks

Prices and payment in U.S. dollars (except for Canadian orders)

1. The Secret Raven: Conflict and Transformation.
Daryl Sharp (Toronto). ISBN 0-919123-00-7. 128 pp. $14
A practical study of *puer* psychology, including dream interpretation and material on midlife crisis, the provisional life, the mother complex, anima and shadow. Illustrated.

2. The Psychological Meaning of Redemption Motifs in Fairytales.
Marie-Louise von Franz (Zurich). ISBN 0-919123-01-5. 128 pp. $14
Unique approach to understanding typical dream motifs (bathing, clothes, animals, etc.).

3. On Divination and Synchronicity: The Psychology of Meaningful Chance.
Marie-Louise von Franz (Zurich). ISBN 0-919123-02-3. 128 pp. $14
Penetrating study of irrational methods of divining fate (I Ching, astrology, palmistry, Tarot cards, etc.), contrasting Western ideas with those of so-called primitives. Illustrated.

4. The Owl Was a Baker's Daughter: Obesity, Anorexia and the Repressed Feminine. Marion Woodman (Toronto). ISBN 0-919123-03-1. 144 pp. $15
A modern classic, with particular attention to the body as mirror of the psyche in weight disturbances and eating disorders. Based on case studies, dreams and mythology. Illus.

5. Alchemy: An Introduction to the Symbolism and the Psychology.
Marie-Louise von Franz (Zurich). ISBN 0-919123-04-X. 288 pp. $18
Detailed guide to what the alchemists were really looking for: emotional wholeness. Invaluable for interpreting images and motifs in modern dreams and drawings. **84 illustrations.**

6. Descent to the Goddess: A Way of Initiation for Women.
Sylvia Brinton Perera (New York). ISBN 0-919123-05-8. 112 pp. $14
A timely and provocative study of the need for an inner, female authority in a masculine-oriented society. Rich in insights from mythology and the author's analytic practice.

7. The Psyche as Sacrament: C.G. Jung and Paul Tillich.
John P. Dourley (Ottawa). ISBN 0-919123-06-6. 128 pp. $14
Comparative study from a dual perspective (author is Catholic priest and Jungian analyst), exploring the psychological meaning of religion, God, Christ, the spirit, the Trinity, etc.

8. Border Crossings: Carlos Castaneda's Path of Knowledge.
Donald Lee Williams (Boulder). ISBN 0-919123-07-4. 160 pp. $15
The first thorough psychological examination of the Don Juan novels, bringing Castaneda's spiritual journey down to earth. Special attention to the psychology of the feminine.

9. Narcissism and Character Transformation. The Psychology of Narcissistic Character Disorders. ISBN 0-919123-08-2. 192 pp. $16
Nathan Schwartz-Salant (New York).
A comprehensive study of narcissistic character disorders, drawing upon a variety of analytic points of view (Jung, Freud, Kohut, Klein, etc.). Theory and clinical material. Illus.

10. Rape and Ritual: A Psychological Study.
Bradley A. Te Paske (Minneapolis). ISBN 0-919123-09-0. 160 pp. $15
Incisive combination of theory, clinical material and mythology. Illustrated.

11. Alcoholism and Women: The Background and the Psychology.
Jan Bauer (Montreal). ISBN 0-919123-10-4. 144 pp. $15
Sociology, case material, dream analysis and archetypal patterns from mythology.

12. Addiction to Perfection: The Still Unravished Bride.
Marion Woodman (Toronto). ISBN 0-919123-11-2. 208 pp. $17
A powerful and authoritative look at the psychology of modern women. Examines dreams, mythology, food rituals, body imagery, sexuality and creativity. A continuing best-seller since its original publication in 1982. Illustrated.

13. Jungian Dream Interpretation: A Handbook of Theory and Practice.
James A. Hall, M.D. (Dallas). ISBN 0-919123-12-0. 128 pp. $14
A practical guide, including common dream motifs and many clinical examples.

14. The Creation of Consciousness: Jung's Myth for Modern Man.
Edward F. Edinger, M.D. (Los Angeles). ISBN 0-919123-13-9. 128 pp. $14
Insightful study of the meaning and purpose of human life. Illustrated.

15. The Analytic Encounter: Transference and Human Relationship.
Mario Jacoby (Zurich). ISBN 0-919123-14-7. 128 pp. $14
Sensitive exploration of the difference between relationships based on projection and I-Thou relationships characterized by mutual respect and psychological objectivity.

16. Change of Life: Psychological Study of Dreams and the Menopause.
Ann Mankowitz (Santa Fe). ISBN 0-919123-15-5. 128 pp. $14
A moving account of an older woman's Jungian analysis, dramatically revealing the later years as a time of rebirth, a unique opportunity for psychological development.

17. The Illness That We Are: A Jungian Critique of Christianity.
John P. Dourley (Ottawa). ISBN 0-919123-16-3. 128 pp. $14
Radical study by Catholic priest and analyst, exploring Jung's qualified appreciation of Christian symbols and ritual, while questioning the masculine ideals of Christianity.

18. Hags and Heroes: A Feminist Approach to Jungian Therapy with Couples.
Polly Young-Eisendrath (Philadelphia). ISBN 0-919123-17-1. 192 pp. $16
Highly original integration of feminist views with the concepts of Jung and Harry Stack Sullivan. Detailed strategies and techniques, emphasis on feminine authority.

19. Cultural Attitudes in Psychological Perspective.
Joseph Henderson , M.D. (San Francisco). ISBN 0-919123-18-X. 128 pp. $14
Shows how a psychological attitude can give depth to one's world view. Illustrated.

21. The Pregnant Virgin: A Process of Psychological Transformation.
Marion Woodman (Toronto). ISBN 0-919123-20-1. 208 pp. $17
A celebration of the feminine, in both men and women. Explores the wisdom of the body, eating disorders, relationships, dreams, addictions, etc. Illustrated.

23. The Scapegoat Complex: Toward a Mythology of Shadow and Guilt.
Sylvia Brinton Perera (New York). ISBN 0-919123-22-8. 128 pp. $14
A hard-hitting study of victim psychology in modern men and women, based on case material, mythology and archetypal patterns.

24. The Bible and the Psyche: Individuation Symbolism in the Old Testament.
Edward F. Edinger (Los Angeles). ISBN 0-919123-23-6. 176 pp. $16
A major new work relating significant Biblical events to the psychological movement toward wholeness that takes place in individuals.

25. The Spiral Way: A Woman's Healing Journey.
Aldo Carotenuto (Rome). ISBN 0-919123-24-4. 144 pp. $15
Detailed case history of a fifty-year-old woman's Jungian analysis, with particular attention to her dreams and the rediscovery of her enthusiasm for life.

26. The Jungian Experience: Analysis and Individuation.
James A. Hall, M.D. (Dallas). ISBN 0-919123-25-2. 176 pp. $16
Comprehensive study of the theory and clinical application of Jungian thought, including Jung's model, the structure of analysis, where to find an analyst, training centers, etc.

27. Phallos: Sacred Image of the Masculine.
Eugene Monick (Scranton/New York). ISBN 0-919123-26-0. 144 pp. $15
Uncovers the essence of masculinity (as opposed to the patriarchy) through close examination of the physical, mythological and psychological aspects of phallos. 30 illustrations.

28. The Christian Archetype: A Jungian Commentary on the Life of Christ.
Edward F. Edinger, M.D. (Los Angeles). ISBN 0-919123-27-9. 144 pp. $15
Psychological view of images and events central to the Christian myth, showing their symbolic meaning in terms of personal individuation. 31 illustrations.

30. Touching: Body Therapy and Depth Psychology.
Deldon Anne McNeely (Lynchburg, VA). ISBN 0-919123-29-5. 128 pp. $14
Illustrates how these two disciplines, both concerned with restoring life to an ailing human psyche, may be integrated in theory and practice. Focus on the healing power of touch.

31. Personality Types: Jung's Model of Typology.
Daryl Sharp (Toronto). ISBN 0-919123-30-9. 128 pp. $14
Detailed explanation of Jung's model (basis for the widely-used Myers-Briggs Type Indicator), showing its implications for individual development and for relationships. Illus.

32. The Sacred Prostitute: Eternal Aspect of the Feminine.
Nancy Qualls-Corbett (Birmingham). ISBN 0-919123-31-7. 176 pp. $16
Shows how our vitality and capacity for joy depend on rediscovering the ancient connection between spirituality and passionate love. Illustrated. (Foreword by Marion Woodman.)

33. When the Spirits Come Back.
Janet O. Dallett (Seal Harbor, WA). ISBN 0-919123-32-5. 160 pp. $15
An analyst examines herself, her profession and the limitations of prevailing attitudes toward mental disturbance. Interweaving her own story with descriptions of those who come to her for help, she details her rediscovery of the integrity of the healing process.

34. The Mother: Archetypal Image in Fairy Tales.
Sibylle Birkhäuser-Oeri (Zurich). ISBN 0-919123-33-3. 176 pp. $16
Compares processes in the unconscious with common images and motifs in folk-lore. Illustrates how positive and negative mother complexes affect us all, with examples from many well-known fairy tales and daily life. (Edited by Marie-Louise von Franz.)

35. The Survival Papers: Anatomy of a Midlife Crisis.
Daryl Sharp (Toronto). ISBN 0-919123-34-1. 160 pp. $15
Jung's major concepts—persona, shadow, anima and animus, complexes, projection, typology, active imagination, individuation, etc.—are dramatically presented in the immediate context of an analysand's process. And the analyst's.

36. The Cassandra Complex: Living with Disbelief.
Laurie Layton Schapira (New York). ISBN 0-919123-35-X. 160 pp. $15
Shows how unconscious, prophetic sensibilities can be transformed from a burden into a valuable source of conscious understanding. Includes clinical material and an examination of the role of powerfully intuitive, medial women through history. Illustrated.

37. Dear Gladys: The Survival Papers, Book 2.
Daryl Sharp (Toronto). ISBN 0-919123-36-8. 144 pp. $15
An entertaining and instructive continuation of the story begun in *The Survival Papers* (title 35). Part textbook, part novel, part personal exposition.

38. The Phallic Quest: Priapus and Masculine Inflation.
James Wyly (Chicago). ISBN 0-919123-37-6. 128 pp. $14
Case studies, including dreams, showing ways in which one may recognize a split-off priapic complex. Priapus is seen as an apt metaphor for patriarchal inflation.

39. Acrobats of the Gods: Dance and Transformation.
Joan Dexter Blackmer (Concord, MA/Wilmot, NH). ISBN 0-919123-38-4. 128 pp. $14
What is physical consciousness and how is it achieved? What is the connection between psyche and matter? A timely reminder that without the body there can be no soul.

40. Eros and Pathos: Shades of Love and Suffering.
Aldo Carotenuto (Rome). ISBN 0-919123-39-2. 160 pp. $15
Why do we fear love? Why do we hurt those close to us? Is there a connection between love, suffering and creativity? There is treasure in the darkness of love and pain.

Prices and payment (check or money order) in $U.S. (in Canada, $Cdn)
Add Postage/Handling: 1-2 books, $2; 3-4 books, $4; 5-8 books, $7

Complete Catalogue and 36-page SAMPLER free on request

INNER CITY BOOKS
Box 1271, Station Q, Toronto, Canada M4T 2P4